D1461733

 **A SAIGA MINI BOOK**

*Saiga Mini books* cover the field of domesticated animals and birds as well as many outdoor activities. They are written by experts in a concise manner, yet in sufficient depth to enable the reader to keep a pet or pursue a hobby quite successfully. They are illustrated throughout with drawings or photographs thus bringing the subject to life in an interesting manner; especially since many of the photographs are of pets kept by leading breeders or fanciers.

A complete list of titles may be obtained from the publisher.

# GOLDFISH AND KOI

by

FRANK W. ORME

 A SAIGA MINI BOOK

SAIGA PUBLISHING CO. LTD.,
1 Royal Parade, Hindhead, Surrey, England GU26 6TD,
PRODUCED AND PUBLISHED BY TRIPLEGATE LTD.

Photographs and drawings by the author

Typesetting by:
Ebony Typesetting, Nr. Liskeard, Cornwall.

Printed by
Broglia Press, Bournemouth

SAIGA PUBLISHING CO. LTD.,
1 Royal Parade, Hindhead, Surrey GU26 6TD,
England.

# CONTENTS

*Chapter*                                                    *Page*

*List of Monochrome Illustrations*                             VI

1   The Aquarium                                                1

2   The Pond                                                   17

3   Routine Maintenance                                        30

4   Goldfish                                                   34

5   Koi                                                        39

6   Choosing and Buying Fish                                   44

7   Feeding                                                    48

8   Problems and Remedies                                      53

9   Fish Breeding                                              61

10  Fish Shows                                                 68

*Appendix* — List of Societies Books and Magazines            73

COLOUR PLATES

Plate 1 Goldfish *Facing page*                                11

Plate 2 Koi *Facing page*                                     26

v

# BLACK AND WHITE ILLUSTRATIONS

*Figure*                                                    *Page*

| | | |
|---|---|---|
| 1.1 | Water surface areas | 2 |
| 1.2 | Correct and incorrect planting | 8 |
| 1.3 | Vallisneria spiralis torta | 10 |
| 1.4 | Fontinalis | 11 |
| 1.5 | External features of the fish | 16 |
| 2.1 | Section through concrete ponds | 21 |
| 2.2 | Section through 'liner' pond | 21 |
| 2.3 | Water-lily | 23 |
| 4.1 | Koi and Goldfish | 38 |
| 5.1 | Koi | 42 |
| 7.1 | Whiteworm | 49 |
| 7.2 | Daphnia and Cyclops | 51 |
| 7.3 | Tubifex | 52 |
| 8.1 | Argulus and Lernaea | 56 |
| 8.2 | Dragonfly nymph | 59 |
| 8.3 | Water scorpion and Water stick-insect | 60 |
| 9.1 | Fish spawning | 62 |

# CHAPTER 1

# THE AQUARIUM

## PLANNING FOR AN AQUARIUM

Before any fish are acquired, some thought should be given to their accommodation. The globular fish bowl should not even be considered because it is invariably much too small and does not provide a sufficiently large water surface for the well-being of coldwater fish. Indeed, any fish which is to be kept indoors is best accommodated in a rectangular glass aquarium.

The smallest tank that should be considered should not be less than 24 inches long × 12 inches wide (610 × 305 mm) with a depth of 12 to 15 inches (305 to 381 mm); anything smaller than this will be more trouble than it is worth. Within reason, the larger the tank the better; however, it is obvious that the bigger the tank the more it will weigh and this could dictate the most suitable location for the aquarium  Whereas a solid floor would be perfectly safe, a timber boarded floor could be too weak, unless the load is spread to distribute the weight. The easiest method is to place the tank and its stand upon two strong battens that are of sufficient length to span at least two of the floor joists. It must be realised that when set up, with water and gravel, the tank mentioned would weigh at least 175 lbs (79.5 kg).

The rule for calculating the number of coldwater fish that can be kept in a volume of water, stipulates a **maximum of 1 inch (25 mm) of fish, excluding the fins, to each 24 square inches (155 cm²) of water surface.** Under no circumstances should a novice attempt to exceed this calculation. It will be noted that the governing factor is the **area of the water surface**, not the volume, therefore it will be obvious that if the above quoted tank were stood on end, so that its depth

1

became 24 inches (610 mm), it would contain the same amount of water but only have half the surface area, thus the number of fish which could be kept in it would also be halved.

## Location

In the home the aquarium should form an attractive feature and be set at a comfortable viewing height, high enough to avoid the attention of small prying fingers, but not so high that it cannot be easily seen from the comfort of an armchair. Although light will be required if the plants are to make satisfactory growth, it should not be placed in a position which receives sunlight continuously for long periods. Possibly, the ideal position is one that allows only about one hour of sunlight to fall directly upon the aquarium. Too much sunlight will quickly cause the glass to be obscured by a green growth of algae; it may even turn the water green. Hot sun shining on the tank may also cause the water to become too warm. Conversely, too little light will result in the plants dying. However, artificial light can be used to supplement any lack of natural daylight. Coldwater fish can be kept entirely under artificial light, but experience has proved that they do benefit from being allowed a certain amount of natural daylight and, where possible, this should

Figure 1.1

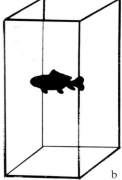

**Water Surface Areas.** Both tanks are identical in size and water capacity, however, (a) has twice the surface area of tank (b) which allows it to accommodate twice as many inches of fish.

be arranged.

Ease of maintenance is another factor that may well govern the position in which the aquarium is to be placed. It is essential that an electric socket should be nearby. Electricity will be required to operate the lights and air pump, and obviously, in the interests of neatness and safety it is better to avoid untidy trailing cables where possible.

At fairly frequent intervals it will be necessary to clean the aquarium by scraping algae off the front glass panel, syphoning accumulated sediment from the surface of the gravel, trimming or replacing plants, removing some of the stale water and replacing with fresh. These tasks are easier to attend to if there is a convenient place to dispose of the dirty water and obtain a fresh supply.

## Type

The choice of aquarium must be a matter of personal preference; however, the larger the aquarium the easier it will be to look after. The greater amount of water is less likely to suffer from sudden fluctuations of temperature, and any pollution problems will take longer to take effect. The attraction of a large aquarium is undeniable if it has a carefully planned underwater scene of rocks and plants, clear water and healthy, active, uncrowded fishes.

Nowadays the 'all–glass' aquarium is the most popular type of tank, and these are available in a range of sizes. Having no frame it allows easy viewing of the interior and aesthetically, is ideal for decorative use in the home. When using this type of aquarium it must always be seated upon a thin layer of polystyrene, such as ceiling tiles, to cushion the base against any unevenness and prevent it cracking.

## FURNISHING THE AQUARIUM

The various elements that go into the aquarium must be given careful consideration, for not only do they affect the final appearance and durability of the miniature underwater world, but they can also have a profound effect upon the well-being of the fish. An attractive looking stone may appear innocent enough but, if placed in the aquarium, it could release poisons causing the fish to die.

## Water

So far as fish are concerned, water is by far the most important element. Known scientifically as $H_2O$, it can be either fresh or salty: fresh water can also be either soft or hard, additionally it nearly always contains some impurities which are normally quite harmless to fish–life. However, some can be a hazard, and high amongst these is the chlorine which Water Authorities add to the domestic water supply. Generally, it is not added in sufficient quantity to harm fish and is easily removed by exposing the water to the fresh air for a few days, or by forcing it, in a jet, through a hose-pipe which will cause the chlorine gas to escape from the water and thus leave it safe. Some writers advise the use of chemicals to nullify the chlorine; but this can be equally harmful.

Fresh water is either neutral, acid or alkaline and these can be measured, the result being known as the pH (potential Hydrogen) value. Neutral water has a reading of 7.07, and readings either side of this figure are either acid or alkaline. Readings of less than 7.07 are acid; the higher the reading above 7.07, the greater the alkaline content. The full range of pH values extends equally on each side of 7.07, graduating from 0.3 up to 14.5. The pH value of water is very easy to ascertain by using one of the various kits that are available from aquatic dealers; a sample of water is taken and a small quantity of a special solution added, the water is then agitated until it changes colour. A comparison of the coloured water against a colour scale will reveal the pH value.

Kits are also available for checking various other qualities of the water, but these are quite unnecessary. If water is drawn from a healthy source, and left to mature for a few days, neither you nor your fish are likely to encounter any problems.

4

## Gravel

The ornamental aquarium will require a strata of gravel in which to root the plants. Silver-sand, red builder's sand, pebbles and stone chippings are all unsuitable; crushed coral is definitely not advised due to its high alkaline content, which can put the fish at risk. Most suitable, and easily obtained, is the aquarium gravel sold by dealers in aquatic stores. Although it is possible to purchase artificially coloured aquarium gravel, it is far better to choose that which is natural. Garishly coloured gravel, like sea–shells and ornaments, have no place in the underwater picture which should resemble a natural underwater scene.

The gravel, of an average depth of 2 inches (5 cm), will need to be thoroughly washed, a little at a time. Place some of the gravel in a washing–up bowl and scald it with boiling water to release any obstinate matter, and then pour off the dirty water. Continue to wash under a stream of running water, pouring off any debris, until the water in the bowl is clear. The washed gravel should be free of any sediment, and this can be checked by placing some of the gravel in a glass jar of water and agitating vigorously. If the water clears immediately after you stop shaking the jar, the gravel is ready for use; if not, it should be given a further wash.

## Rocks

Rockwork can add interest, if kept in proportion, by helping to create a natural underwater scene, but it must blend in with the overall picture and not dominate it. Not all rocks are suitable: some may be soft and will break down and disintegrate with time, others may be dangerous because of their chemical composition. Some sandstones fall into the first category, while limestone and marble must be avoided because of their dangerously high alkaline content which, sooner or later, will prove fatal to the fish. Hard water–worn sandstone, Westmoreland, Somerset, and York rock are quite safe. Granite, slate, tufa and pumice–stone should also be safe to use.

When selecting the rock, study it carefully. It should be well worn with no sharp edges that might damage the fish.

Consider the size and shape of each piece of rock and visualise it in the aquarium. It must be of the right proportions and sit upon a wide base that will prevent it falling over. Obviously if more than one rock is used they should all be of the same type.

## Plants

Plastic plants can be bought but these never look anything but what they are and, serving no useful purpose, should be left out of the aquarium.

There are not as many coldwater plants available as there are for the tropical aquarium; nevertheless, there are enough varieties to suit the demand of most coldwater fishkeepers. Some can be grown in both cold and tropical tanks, so the difficulty is, therefore, to find those which have been grown under cold conditions, for they will stand the best chance of survival in the aquarium. Probably the best place from which to acquire plants is a nursery that specialises in the cultivation of water plants. If it is possible to make a personal visit so much the better, for the conditions under which they have been raised can then be seen; failing that, obtain their catalogue and order through the post. It is also possible to buy plants from a dealer, however, there may not be a very large range to select from.

Avoid plants that appear yellowish or spindly and leggy and try not to choose from plants that are in a tropical aquarium, or heated water. Ideally the plant should be sturdy and a healthy green with a good root system, unless it is a cutting. To obtain the best effects the plants should be grouped in drifts and clusters, as they would be found in Nature, and a suggested minimum number of plants can be based upon one plant to every 4 square inches (26 cm$^2$) of the aquarium base — in other words a 24" × 12" (610 mm × 305 mm) area would require around seventy-two plants. Keep these facts in mind when planning the number of plants of each variety that are to be purchased.

## Role of Plants

Aquarium plants are required to perform a number of

functions; they must be decorative yet sturdy enough to resist the attention of the fish; they must help to oxygenate the water; their roots must purify the gravel; they must absorb impurities. Additionally they must provide a browsing area for the fish; a receptacle for the eggs of spawning fish; and shelter for fry and small fish. If the plants are to perform their task satisfactorily they must receive the correct intensity of light; the planting medium must suit them; the character of the water must be to their liking; and there must be an adequate food supply (this being supplied from the fish droppings).

The novice fishkeeper should not therefore be surprised, or lose heart, if some of the plants fail to do well or die. It is logical that the conditions of the aquarium will not be to the liking of all varieties of plants and these will not flourish; however, other types will be quite happy in the conditions provided by the aquarium. Losses can be made good from the successful plants, or other varieties can be tried. For a time it will be a matter of experimentation until a successful combination of suitable plants is arrived at.

## Plants sold as cuttings

The type of water plants required for the aquarium are known as 'submerged aquatic plants' and the following is a list of the more easily available sorts:

*Elodea canadensis:*
an excellent oxygenator; consists of a much branched stem thickly dressed in narrow lanceolate leaves. Grows well in the company of Vallisneria with which it makes a good contrast. Fast growing plant and makes few demands; but needs bright light if it is to succeed. Sold as cuttings, it propagates and roots quite easily from segments broken from the main stem.

*Elodea densa:*
similar to, but stouter than the previous plant. Sparsely branched single main stem; narrow lanceolate leaves grow into whorls around the stems. Easily grown from cuttings, requires good light intensity to succeed.

*Lagarosiphon muscoides:*
very similar to E. densa; distinctly tubular in appearance. Thick but fragile stem, encircled by dark-green crispate leaves. Given lots of light, especially during the winter months, grows well with *Vallisneria*

and *Ludwigia*. Propagated in the same manner as the *Elodeas*.

## *Ceratophyllum demersum* (Hornwort):

a favourite of many fish keepers. Distinct seasonal cycle, tends to die back in winter. Never develops roots, although may develop a lightish-coloured shoot that will penetrate the gravel; needs anchoring down. The main stem: many–branched, dark green and stiffish, the older portion bare of leaves. Leaves: 'needle–like' in appearance, arranged in whorls around the stems and very brittle; the plant should be handled with care. A good oxygenator, the plant does best at a temperature in the lower 60°F (15°C) region.

## *Myriophyllum spicatum:*

probably a better subject for the aquarium than the previous plant. Also known by the common name of Milfoil; widely spread throughout much of the world. Branched stems carry whorls of four or five feathery, pinnate leaves, olive–green in colour; stems reddish–brown. Propagate from cuttings; forms a strong root system and requires a good intensity of light. Under the right conditions, an excellent oxygenator and will make good growth.

## *Myriophyllum verticillatum:*

another Milfoil which may succeed if the water is a little too acid for the former type. These plants prefer a pH value of 7.5 to 8.0.

Figure 1.2   Correct and Incorrect Planting

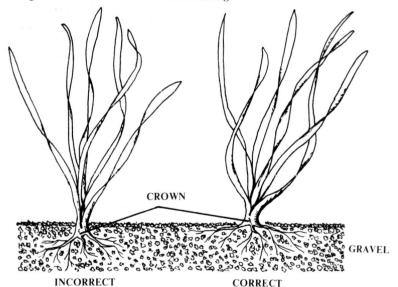

CROWN

GRAVEL

INCORRECT                    CORRECT

*Correct Planting Depth for Submerged Plants*

Rooted plants, particularly vallisneria and sagittaria, should be planted with the crown above the gravel surface to prevent rotting.

8

*Ludwigia palustria:*
a very good contrast plant; will root from cuttings. Thick articulated stem, branching into side–shoots and carrying opposed sessile leaves. Blades, thick and smooth, bright green on the upper surface; underside may be dark green to wine–red. During the winter period it often sheds the lower leaves as part of the vegetative cycle. Allow sufficient light and it should do well in the aquarium.

The above water plants will all be sold as cuttings; buy at least six to form a group. The individual stems should be firmly inserted into the gravel and weighted down. The easiest method is to obtain lead wire from the plant dealer and attach a small strip to the stem: take care that the plant is not bruised as this may cause the stem to rot.

## Rooting Plants

In the case of the following plants they should possess a healthy rooting system. When planting, make a shallow depression, spread out the roots, carefully cover and lightly firm down. An important point to observe is that only the roots should be covered, the growing crown must be kept above the gravel, otherwise the plant may rot. Remember that the success and appearance of the aquarium will rely to a large extent upon the power of the plants to survive and multiply — rough treatment will lessen their ability to adapt to their new environment.

*Sagittaria subulata:*
adapts to a variety of aquarium conditions, popular for this reason. Leaves ribbon–shaped, bent or curved; unlike *Vallisneria*, apex is not dentate. Young plants grow on runners from the short root–stock of the parent. Establishes itself fairly readily in a poorer lit position, thus a good background plant. Three forms: *gracillima*, leaves about 3 feet (915 cm) long; *natans* form floating leaves, the underwater leaves around 12–13 inches (305–330 mm) long; *pusilla*, the smallest form with leaves approximately 4 inches (102 mm) in length and can, therefore, be kept towards front of aquarium.

*Vallisneria spiralis:*
similar, in some respects, to *Sagittaria*. Leaves, grass–like, and arise from a short root–stock from which runners grow to develop young plants; ribbon-shaped and reach length of 8 to 36 inches (203-915 mm) terminating in a tiny dentation in the tip. An old, long–established aquarium plant which can adapt to a variety of conditions. An

excellent background plant giving the aquarium realistic look. Likes plenty of light, especially sunlight.

*V. torta*

has spiralling twists to the leaves. An attractive plant but not as hardy in the coldwater tank as spiralis.

**Eleocharis acicularis** (Hair Grass):

if it takes to the aquarium, unfortunately it does not accept all conditions, it forms a carpet of green, with its thread–like 'foliage'. Filiform stalks arise from a creeping root–stock to form tufts. Each grass–like stalk develops tiny bunches of roots and is self–supporting.

**Fontinalis antipyretica:**

not a rooting plant, but a water moss with branched stems and leaves. Leaves fit closely around the stem; dark olive–green to brownish in colour. Usually found in cool flowing water attached to solid objects. If collected from the wild it must be thoroughly and carefully cleaned and sterilized to rid it of parasites. If possible, transfer both moss and object to which it is attached. Has the habit of attracting sediment and may require frequent swillings.

**Floating plants** can, and often do, become a nuisance and, for this reason, are better left out of the aquarium.

Figure 1.3    Vallisneria spiralis torta.

10

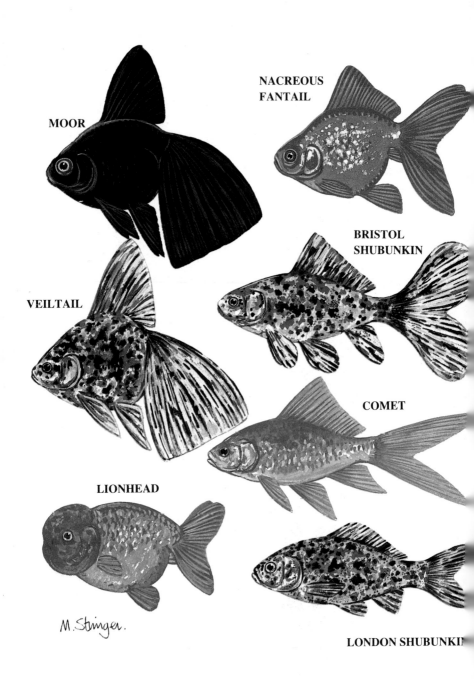

MOOR

NACREOUS
FANTAIL

BRISTOL
SHUBUNKIN

VEILTAIL

COMET

LIONHEAD

M. Stinger.

LONDON SHUBUNKIN

**Plate 1**  Goldfish

## Cleaning

All plants should be carefully cleaned before they are placed into their growing position. First rinse them and remove any suspicious matter, such as the jelly–like egg cases of snails. Yellow and dead leaves should be gently taken from the plant, at the same time cleaning up the roots. They must then be sterilized to kill the many unwelcome pests and parasites which may have escaped the cleaning process. Make a weak solution of potassium permanganate by dissolving adequate crystals in hot water to turn a bowl of water to a pale-pink colour and allow to cool. Place the plants in this solution to soak for two to three hours. Finally, wash under running water, by gently rubbing the leaves and stems between the thumb and finger, before placing the plants into a bowl of clean water. Rocks obtained from below water may be cleaned and sterilised in

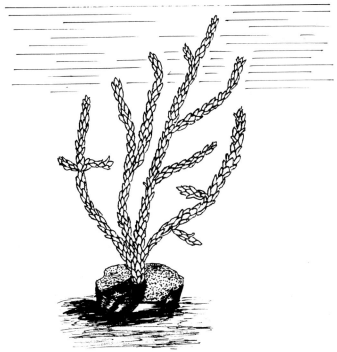

Figure 1.4 **Fontinalis**

11

the same manner.

Cleanliness must be exercised at all times in fishkeeping. Fail to practice cleanliness and all sorts of problems can, and probably will, arise.

## Filters

Before the advent of filters, the old–time aquarist would now have all that was necessary to commence fishkeeping; an aquarium, clean gravel, sterilized rocks and plants. However, the modern aquarist prefers to incorporate some form of filter system. Probably the most trouble–free type is that known as an 'under–gravel filter.' Under–gravel filters consist of perforated plates, or a grid of perforated plastic tubes, which are laid on the bottom of the aquarium and covered over with the gravel. The filter is connected by flexible plastic tubing to an air pump; when operating, water is drawn through the gravel bed carrying with it any matter which is suspended in the water, thus helping to preserve the clarity of the water. This method of filtration relies, to some extent, upon the action of bacteria which forms within the gravel. The movement of the water through the gravel, bringing with it the matter and dissolved oxygen, promotes the growth of the bacterial colony which, in turn, breaks down the suspended matter and renders it safe – the end product providing food for the plants. Once the colony has formed and reached maximum efficiency it will continue to purify the water for a long period of time, provided that the filter is allowed to run continuously; however, if the air pump is switched off for too long the colony will die.

### SETTING UP

Having considered the elements which will go into the tank, the tank can now be furnished to create an ideal home. Despite any eager impatience to see the aquarium planted, and the fish in place, this should not be hurried. An aquarium that has been hastily planted stands little chance of becoming an object of attraction, whereas patience and careful planning will bring rewards and provide a great deal of pleasure for many years to come.

12

## Layout

Make a few sketches of possible layouts for the interior of the tank, selecting the best position for any rockwork and commit the idea to paper. Decide where to put plants, and their variety. Mark down the clumps and drifts; arrange the plants around the rocks; study the drawings and revise to reach the best design. If the drawings are made to scale it will be possible to estimate how many of each type of plant is required. This is no different to the methods employed by a professional gardener when planning a garden layout — how much more important it is when creating a miniature world in which creatures will live!

Clean the tank thoroughly to remove all traces of dirt, smudges or smears, then dry it to a sparkling clarity and place upon its stand. Finally, make sure that it is level in all directions, with a spirit level.

If 'under-gravel' filtration is to be used the unit should be installed at this stage. Arrange the perforated plates, or tubes, to cover the base according to the manufacturer's instructions. Measure the amount of flexible tube required to reach from the filter to the air pump. Cut the required length and attach it to the filter air-lift tube — drape the other end over the top of the tank so that it will be out of the way of further operations.

The carefully cleaned gravel can now be placed into the tank **a little at a time**; not the whole lot in one go. Spread the gravel evenly, building a slope from the back down to the front, which should be about 1 inch deep (25 mm) at its lowest point. By arranging a slope the sediment will tend to gather at the low point, from where it can easily be syphoned out. Next the well-cleaned rocks can be put into position; move the pieces around until they look right and appear natural, and when you are satisfied, carefully ease them down into the gravel, so that they look as though they have always been there. Smooth the gravel surface and lightly firm it with the palm of the hand. Do not bother to form artistic undulations, because the fish will only level them out by their habit of rooting in the gravel. The reason for bedding the rocks into the gravel, apart from giving them an appearance of permanency, is to prevent uneaten food or other matter getting trapped beneath them.

### Filling the Tank

This is not merely a case of pouring the water in, as to do so would swirl the gravel around and undo all of the previous work. First cover the gravel with a sheet of newspaper and stand a deepish plate on this. Water can now be poured slowly into the plate from where it will overflow onto the paper. Provided the water is not poured fast, the newspaper will protect the gravel from disturbance, despite the fact that the paper may float up around the plate as the water level rises. When the tank is about three parts full the plate and paper can be removed. Within a short time it is quite possible that small bubbles will form upon the glass and rock surfaces; this is excess, undissolved oxygen. However, they will slowly disappear either by absorption into the water or by being dispelled into the atmosphere. Allow the tank to stand for a day or two, to settle down, after which the gravel can be carefully syphoned over to remove any traces of settled sediment.

If it is intended to incorporate an **air–stone** it should be done before planting. Cut sufficient flexible plastic tube to reach from the air pump, run down a rear corner and pass it, beneath the gravel, to the air–stone, which should be hidden behind one of the rocks. Hiding the air–stone and tubing will avoid the intrusion of any artificiality in what, it is hoped, will appear to be a natural, even if miniature, section of a pond or stream.

### Planting

This completes the scene and must, therefore, be treated with careful attention to detail. Plant in natural groups and drifts, trying to screen the rear corner angles. Study the effect as each group is planted and alter the plants until you are quite satisfied with the result. Continue until the plants have all been positioned, carefully checking the appearance of the growing picture to ensure the completed scene looks natural and pleasing.

Refill the tank by placing a sheet of newspaper over the lowered water surface and gently pour water onto it. Remove the paper, and wipe away any spilled water or splashes; connect the flexible tubes to the air-pump and quickly check that it works.

A **cover glass** can be placed across the top of the tank to prevent dust falling in and to deter any would-be interference. The glass should be so arranged that it leaves a slight air–gap to allow a free circulation of air over the surface of the water.

## Lighting

A lighting hood can be stood upon the cover glass to provide any additional light to the interior. The amount of artificial light required to maintain the health of the plants is important and approximately determinable by multiplying the length of the tank by $3\frac{1}{4}$. This gives the wattage necessary to light the interior for ten hours each day. The calculation is made in inches and applies to tungsten light sources, either bulb or strip, and must be divided by 4 to arrive at the figure for fluorescent light. It then becomes a matter of trial and error to get the best combination of light intensity and duration; this is not difficult, it relies upon observation — noting the results produced and adjusting the time/light intensity accordingly, until the most suitable conditions are achieved.

The ideal to aim for is where the various plants grow and produce sturdy new green growth, but the algae remains within reasonable bounds and does not discolour the water or cover the interior in an unsightly green blanket. Unfortunately, even when the correct lighting condition is found it will not suit every plant; some need more light than others, and some are bound to fail. However, it is a simple matter to replace the failures with those which find the conditions agreeable.

In order to allow the plants to root themselves and become established, the aquarium should be allowed to settle down for at least seven days before any fish are introduced —

otherwise it is quite likely that the plants will soon be uprooted.

## SNAILS

It is often suggested that snails should be introduced; however, they are better left out. Many will attack the living plants, and they will proliferate. Despite what some may say, fish will seldom eat snail eggs.

Snails are the intermediate hosts of fish parasites and may well pollute the water.

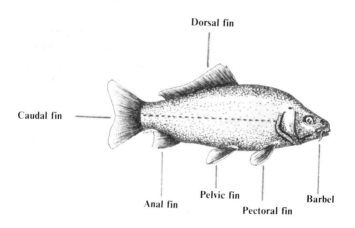

Figure 1.5   **External Features of Fish**

# CHAPTER 2

# THE POND

## PLANNING AND CONSTRUCTION

A larger pond is less trouble than a small pool, and again, pond plants require light in exactly the same way as those in an aquarium. For these reasons, it is sensible to give some thought to the size and position of the proposed pond. It is not enough merely to dig a hole, in some out-of-the-way part of the garden, line it with some form of waterproof material, and fill it with water. To be a success a pond must be planned with care.

The right position must be chosen, the size and shape well thought out, and the construction executed with care. When completed it should become a focal point that attracts the eye; on the other hand, a badly sited, shoddily made pond will forever be a nuisance; an offence to both man and Nature!

### Size and Location

Koi demand a larger pond than would be required for goldfish. The shape of the pond will be a matter of personal preference, but it should be in a position which allows it to receive plenty of daylight. It would be difficult to bring light to a pond which has been built in a situation that is permanently in the shade; it is, on the other hand, always possible to devise a means of shading a pond which receives too much light.

Avoid placing a pond in the near vicinity of trees, for their roots can cause damage and the leaves will fall into the water and cause pollution of the water to the danger of the fish. The leaves of laburnum, laurel, holly and rhododendrons

17

are toxic to fish; in particular, the seeds of the laburnum are very dangerous — they contain the water–soluble alkaloid 'cystine', which is poisonous to man and fish.

## Shape

**Ornamental ponds** may be formal or informal in shape; they may be sunk flush with the surrounding land or raised by being built on the land surface; or they may be part below and part above ground level. My own preference is for the latter type which allows a low wall to form part of the structure; an ideal place to sit and, more importantly it acts as a safety barrier, preventing small children falling into the water.

**Formal ponds** may be square, rectangular, circular or oval in shape. Such a pond is really only suitable for a formally designed garden where it will be complemented by the straight lines of precision–cut hedges, regimented herbaceous and rose gardens, and similar situations where the lines of formality reign.

The true **informal pond** requires an informal setting of natural outlines and curves, semi–wild planting of gardens, and an avoidance of straight lines. The grounds, although tended, should not be obviously created but, instead, appear a creation of Nature. Such settings are not normally encountered in the smaller modern gardens of our times.

As a rule, modern housing estates tend to have smallish gardens and this somewhat restricts the style of garden design. Probably the most popular shape nowadays is a variation of the kidney outline. This design can almost always be adapted to blend in with modern garden layout, being almost infinitely variable.

Whatever the shape of the pond it must always be wider than it is deep. This depth may be as much as 4 feet (1.22 m), but should not be less than 18 inches (41.7 cm). Where the water is liable to freeze during cold weather the depth could, with advantage, be in the region of 3 feet (91.4 cm), to allow a safety margin for the fish. In fact, the well designed pond will provide a shallow area as well as a deep one.

There is no such thing as the perfect design or size for a

pond. The answer is to allow the largest water surface compatible with the size of the garden. Possibly anything with a surface area less than 30 square feet (2.8 m²) is hardly worth the effort required to construct it.

The sensible way to decide the correct size and shape to suit a particular garden, and ensure that it blends in, is to draw a sketch. With a pencil sketch onto paper the boundaries and main features of the garden; if graph paper is used the drawing can be made to scale. Make a cut-out of the proposed pond shape, cutting the size to scale, and try this in various positions to decide the best one and correct proportion. When a satisfactory size, shape and location have been arrived at, it can be roughly marked out, life-size, by pouring sand (or even white flour) to the outline of the pond in its proposed position; if any slight alterations are thought necessary the line can be brushed out and re-marked.

## Digging the hole

Ideally ponds should be constructed during a cool, dry, settled spell of weather. Rain will create a muddy quagmire, and thus unpleasurable working conditions, as will hot sun or cold wind.

The method of digging out the hole is a matter for the labourer, and it will be hard labour! If the excavation is to be very large it may well be worthwhile considering the hire of a mechanical digger. Although expensive it will save many hours of very hard work and so justify its cost. Shape the excavation, as work proceeds, into the desired form of the finished pond, with its deep and shallow areas.

Before beginning construction, decide where the large amount of excavated soil is to be put. The amount of soil will be considerable and should be deposited well away from the scene of operations, so that it does not impede the progress of the worker. Subsequently, if desired, it can be used as the basis of a raised rockery — if this is the intention, be sure to keep the fertile top 6 inches separate.

## Plant shelving

Provision must be made for the plants by arranging shelves when constructing the pond. If it is intended to put the plants in containers the shelves must be so positioned that the depth of the containers plus the growing length of the plants is allowed for. Where plants are to be grown in a permanent position in the pond the shelves must contain lips capable of holding a 3–4 inch (76–102 mm) depth of compost in position. The thickest area of submerged water plants, and thus the greatest area of shelving, should be at the shallow end of the pond. The fish prefer to spawn in shallow water and, as the water is usually warmer, young fish will congregate in the shallows and be protected by the growth of vegetation. Unfortunately, fish are cannibalistic and will eat their own eggs and any fish small enough to be caught. Even with the protection of plants many young fish will be lost — without them it is doubtful whether any would survive.

## Pond liners

At one time most ponds were constructed in concrete, however, the modern method is to use a liner. There are, broadly speaking, three types of pond liners. The cheapest and least satisfactory is polythene. **Polythene** has the great disadvantage of deteriorating after a few years; it tends to rot above the water line where it is exposed to the sun and air. If cost is a serious consideration choose 500 gauge black polythene as this has a somewhat longer life than the clear type. Nylon mesh reinforced **PVC** is a better alternative. This is a tougher type of liner which wears well and has a greater resistance to being punctured. **Butyl** liners are the best of all, because the material is very tough and it has an indefinite life. Butyl has an advantage in that it can be joined by electric welding, or by the use of a special adhesive and tape, which allows various shapes to be created.

Being flexible, plastic liners are not affected by ground movement, freezing, or the effects of contraction and expansion caused by temperature fluctuations.

In order to determine the size of liner required, the length and width should be measured. Measure from the top edge of one wall, down to and along the base and up to the top edge of the opposing wall. Both measurements must then have an additional 24 inches (610 mm) added to them, this is to allow a 12 inch (305 mm) overlap all round, which will be covered by the surround.

Having prepared the excavation, carefully remove any sharp stones or other material that might puncture the liner. Next lay a 2-inch layer (51 mm) of soft sand over the bottom; the alternative is to line the excavation with several sheets of old newspapers. Lay the liner over the excavation, allowing it to sag into the hole, checking that there is an equal overlap all round. Place a few bricks, or other weights, around the overlap to hold it in position.

Figure 2.1   **Section through concrete ponds.**

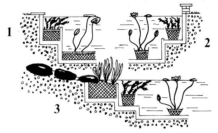

1. Ground level pond with paved surround. Gravel covered loam in planting trough and on base.
2. Dwarf wall surround. Gravel covered loam in baskets.
3. Pond with rockery and bog area.

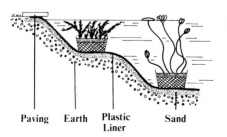

Paving     Earth     Plastic     Sand
                     Liner

Figure 2.2   **Section through 'liner' pond with paved edge.**

21

The pond can now be slowly filled with water. As the weight of the water pulls the liner down, and moulds it to the shape of the pond, gently pull and ease the liner into position to try to disguise any folds or creases that may form. Care at this stage will add much to the appearance of the finished pond.

Although the overlap may be hidden by turves it is far better to lay paving; this will make a firm area for standing on during inclement weather. Flatten the liner overhang onto the surrounding ground, lay mortar upon this and bed the paving down, allowing a slight overhang at the edge of the pond.

**Fibreglass** pools are preformed shells, available in many shapes and sizes, unfortunately they are seldom deep enough to provide truly safe winter protection for any fishes. Installation merely requires a suitable size hole, into which the shell is placed and levelled; it is then infilled to hold it firm.

## PLANTS

Although many people plant the underwater vegetation directly into the pond it is preferable, especially with the average sized pond, to place the plants into containers.

### Varieties

Probably the most popular plant for ponds is the **water–lily**, which can be had in a range of varieties and colours. To obtain a comprehensive catalogue of these beautiful plants, a subject that could fill a book, one of the specialist water–plant nurseries should be contacted or, better still, visited to see the varieties which are available and the conditions in which they are being grown. The following is no more than a list of the more easily obtainable types listed according to the depth of water which best suits them. Many water–lilies which prefer deep water may also succeed in shallower water, although they may well overpower a smaller type pond. However, water–lilies which normally grow in shallow water seldom do well in deep water.

**Depth 6″–12″ (152–305 mm)**
 *Candida*, white with a yellow centre; *Laydekeri lilacina*, pink; *Froebelii*, bright red; *Graziella*, reddish–copper turning to orange–yellow; *Pink Opal*, deep coral pink; *Pygmaea helvola*, yellow.

**Depth 12″–24″ (305–610 mm)**
 *Albatross*, white; *Escarboucle*, crimson; *Esmerelda*, rose–white, mottled and striped deep-rose; *Marliacea alba*, white; *Sunrise*, yellow; *Sultan*, cherry–red, stained white; *Vesuve*, purply–red.

**Depth 24″–36″ (610–915 mm)**
 *Nuphar lutea*, yellow; *Nymphaea alba*, white, the common water–lily; *Picciola*, amaranth–crimson; *Virginalis*, snowy–white.

Prior to planting, all dead leaves and stems should be removed and the roots trimmed. Cleaning and sterilizing must then be attended to.

The *Odorata* and *Tuberosa* types have long fleshy rhizomes which should be set under 1 inch (2.5 cm) of the planting medium, leaving the crown only just exposed. Tubers of the *Marliacae* group are large and rounded with fibrous roots, these should be planted vertically with the roots well spread and the crown above the medium. The *Laydekeri* group have

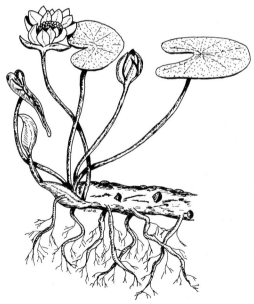

Figure 2.3 **Water lily**

23

a similar, but smaller root–stock to *Marliacea* and are best set in a semi–horizontal position with the crown exposed.

**Planting** is best carried out between May and June, when the plant is starting to grow. Water–lilies may be planted directly into the pond or in containers. *Container planting* is the better method for the average pond, because it allows easy removal for trimming when cleaning the pond. Moulded plastic containers are available in various colours and sizes, specifically manufactured for water–lilies. Mix a small amount of bonemeal into a good turfy loam for the planting medium, and soak well after it has been firmed into the bed or container. The water–lily can then be planted, but weight the tuber down lightly to prevent it breaking loose and floating to the water surface. After planting it should either be lowered gradually to the bottom of the pond over a period of time or covered with around 6 inches (152 mm) of water. As the water–lily grows, slowly increase the depth over a period of weeks.

Thinning out and propagation is by division of the root–stock during April and May. A sharp knife should be used to cut the tough rhizomes; each crown must be left with several inches of the tuber attached, and then planted in the normal way.

The choice of **other aquatic plants**, for the pond, is not over plentiful, however any of the following should prove suitable:

*Aponogeton distachyus* (Water hawthorn):
   originating from South Africa; has long been established in cooler climates. Sweet vanilla–like fragrance, which delightfully perfumes the evening air. Similar mode of growth to the water–lily; elongated ovoidish leaves that float upon the water surface — green leaves are mottled with purplish–brown blotches. A forked spike carries the flowers, snow–white with coal–black anthers. Plant in the same way as the water–lily at any depth from 6 inches up to 2 feet (152–610 mm).

*Callitriche palustris* (Starwort):
   enjoys cold water and spreads rapidly. Underwater leaves, linear; floating leaves lanceolate and form a rosette on the surface. Cuttings root quite easily.

*Ranunculus aquatilis* (Water crowfoot):
   the submerged leaves finely divided into stiff hair–like segments; floating leaves, kidney–shaped, divided into three lobes and three

leaflets. White flowers have a yellow patch at the base; borne on upright stalks above water surface. Propagation of cuttings not difficult.

*Hottonia palustris* (Water violet):

another flowering plant; bears lilac–tinted spikes of flowers above water surface. Fern–like leaves, pinnately pretinated into linear cuts growing upon alternate branched stems. Enjoys cold water and forms winter buds (turion). Propagate by division of root–stock.

Additionally, those plants mentioned as suitable for the aquarium can lend themselves to the underwater scene of the pond.

The rate of planting should be upon the basis of around twenty–four to each square foot of the bottom area of the pond; this should be sufficient to keep the water reasonably clear once they have become established.

## Marginal plants

Also useful for growing around the shallow edges of the pond are those plants known as 'marginal plants'. There are a large number of plants in this class, but only the more popular will be mentioned here. They will grow in conditions which range from having their roots covered by 6 inches of water to those where the soil is merely wet, all they ask is that their roots are kept moist and not allowed to dry out.

Do not grow too many different kinds or the effect will be lost. A few of each, grouped together, will look far more pleasing. By the same token, select types that are in keeping with the size of the pond. A small pond surrounded by some of the larger, tall growing, marginals will look completely wrong, and small plants of little height around a large pond would be very insignificant.

Plant firmly; if necessary weight the plant until the roots have taken a grip, and try not to plant deeper than the pale bottom portion which shows the depth at which it has been growing.

*Acorus calamus* (Sweet Flag):

grows to 3 feet (915 mm); scented; small yellowish flowers during June–July.

25

*Butomus umbellatus* (Flowering Rush):
> height 2-4 feet (610-1219 mm); sword-shaped leaves; umbels of small rose-pink flowers during June–August.

*Calla palustris* (Bog Arum):
> height 6–9 inches (152–229 mm); heart-shaped leaves; creeping root-stock; white arum–like flowers April–June.

*Caltha palustris* (Marsh Marigold):
> grows to 1 foot (305 mm); heart-shaped leaves; butter-yellow flowers during April–May.

*Iris laevigata:*
> height 2 feet (610 mm); sword-shaped leaves; white flowers June–September, if of the *Alba* variety; the common form has blue flowers.

*Iris pseudacorus:*
> height $2\frac{1}{2}$ feet (762 mm); similar to the previous iris, the colour of its flowers depending upon the variety.

*Juncus effusus spiralis* (Corkscrew Rush):
> 18 inch (457 mm) twisted stems; *vittatus* has 3 feet (915 mm) high leaves with yellow stripes.

*Mentha aquatica* (Water Mint):
> height 1–4 feet (305–1219 mm); lilac flowers during August and September.

*Myosotis scorpioides* (Forget-me-not):
> height 9–12 inches (229–305 mm); sky-blue flowers May–July.

*Pontederia cordata* (Pickerel Weed):
> height 2 feet (610 mm); arrow-shaped leaves on long stems; blue flower spikes during summer months.

*Sagittaria sagittifolia* (Common Arrowhead):
> height 18 inches (457 mm); white flowers during mid–summer.

*Scirpus albescens:*
> variegated green and white stems rising to 3 feet (915 mm).

*Typha minima:*
> a small reedmace with rusty pistillates, growing to $1\frac{1}{2}$ feet (457 mm).

Apart from occasional thinning to prevent any over-crowding, these plants only need cutting down at the end of the season, to remove the dead foliage and keep them tidy.


FILLING THE POND

After placing the pond and marginal plants into position the pond will require filling. Do not be over-anxious; hurried action at this stage can quickly undo all the care which has been taken, as rushing jets of water from a hose-pipe may well disturb the planting medium and create clouds of mud and, possibly, uproot the plants. If that should happen it will be necessary to clean out the pond and

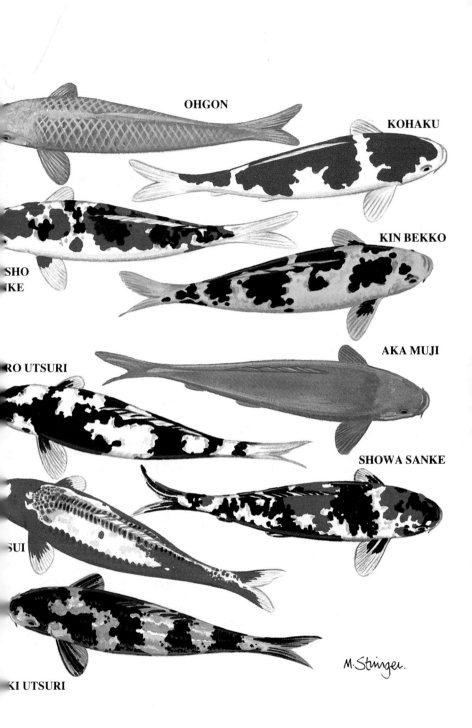

OHGON

KOHAKU

KIN BEKKO

SHO
KE

AKA MUJI

RO UTSURI

SHOWA SANKE

SUI

M. Stringer.

KI UTSURI

**Plate 2** Koi

replant it. Allow the pond to stand for a week or so, to give the plants time to take a firm grip. It should then be emptied, and flushed out to remove any sediment, and refilled, after which it should again be left for a few days before introducing any fish.

## Pumps

Many people like to have a fountain operating in the pond, however, fountains should only find a place in the formal pond. Moving water is certainly an attraction, and benefits the pond and its occupants, although water–lilies prefer still water. Waterfalls look far more natural and are not difficult to arrange. But, be it a fountain or a waterfall, a pump will be required in order to lift the water.

Water pumps generally fall into two categories; the **surface type** and the **submersible**. Within these two categories there is a wide range in price, and output power, for the different models.

The easiest type of pump to install is the **submersible**, which may operate direct from the main electric power supply or through a transformer. It is placed in the pond, below water, and connected to whatever it is to operate. After connecting to the power supply, and switching on, it will immediately begin to work without further ado.

The more costly and, usually, more powerful **surface type** pump is placed outside the pond in a specially constructed housing or chamber as near to the water as possible. The chamber should be weatherproof and allow the pump to be lower than the water level of the pond, at the same time it must be built in such a way that any water can easily drain away, thus preventing the pump from being drowned.

Consider the amount of work which the pump will be required to perform and the volume of water it must turn over within a given time, then select the pump which most nearly meets those requirements. Always err on the generous side by choosing a slightly more powerful pump, rather than a pump of lower capacity and power, so that it does not have to work beyond its capabilities.

**Filters**

If desired, the pond can be filtered, indeed the majority of koi–keepers insist upon having some form of filtration to preserve the clarity of their often plant–free ponds.

One method, but expensive, is to install the type of filter used in the filtration of outdoor swimming pools, following the maker's instructions. These are usually known as 'high rate sand filters' and use silica sand as the filter medium. They are, of course, very efficient, but they require a powerful, high capacity pump to operate a sufficiently high through–flow of water.

An alternative, which may be used in conjunction with the swimming pool filter, is to construct an 'under gravel filter' similar to those used in aquariums. Ideally, if this latter system is to be used, the pond should be constructed to allow 12–18 inches (305–457 mm) greater depth than would otherwise be required.

The filter should cover an area not less than one third of the surface area of the pond. With rigid plastic $\frac{3}{4}$ inch (19 mm) bore pipe, 'tee' pieces and elbows, construct a frame to the required size. The straight lengths should be drilled with $\frac{1}{4}$ inch (6 mm) holes; the distance between holes should gradually lessen the further they are from the pump connection point. Make the connecting point by inserting into the frame a 'tee' piece to which a length of flexible hosepipe has been joined. Space the long pipes about 8 inches (203 mm) apart.

Lay the frame in position on the bottom of the pond and connect it to the pump. The perforated frame should then be covered to a depth of 18 inches (457 mm) with well–washed $\frac{3}{4}$ inch (19 mm) screened gravel. The filter is then ready to operate. The pump to be used should be able to produce a water flow rate through the filter of about 10 gallons (45.5 litres) per hour, although, depending upon the size of the pond and number of fishes, this may have to be increased. However, it must be capable of continuous running to be fully effective — a state which the filter will not achieve until it has been operating for a time.

Very large ponds may require a more sophisticated form

of filtration. These are large water–tight containers, set above the water level of the pond, which interconnect. In general each container has an internal measurement of approximately that of a 30 inch (762 mm) cube. Large diameter pipes lead from the near top of one container to the bottom of the next, allowing water to enter at the bottom and discharge from the top. Each of the filter chambers contains washed coke, which is graded from large pieces in the first container to smaller pieces in the final chamber. Usually the system comprises three to four chambers, and is set alongside the pond.

A powerful pump is used to lift the pond–water into the first chamber, from there it percolates up through the coke and enters the next chamber to repeat the process through to the last container, before returning to the pond.

The output from these filter systems, whether used individually or combined, can be connected to a waterfall which will be beneficial, as it aerates filtered water upon its return to the pond.

## Stocking

Delay stocking the pond for two or three weeks, until the plants have settled down and/or the filter system is operating in a satisfactory manner. Snails and mussels are not desirable residents and are better excluded. Ideally the best time to plant, and stock, a pond is during the early spring.

# CHAPTER 3

## ROUTINE MAINTENANCE

### MAINTAINING BALANCE OF LIFE

In nature each form of life fights for dominance, in one way or another. Strong–growing plants try to crowd out the weaker types; creature preys upon creature, each intent upon survival; only an uneasy balance is reached. However, that is not the sort of ruthless balance desirable in the aquarium or pond; therefore it is necessary to exercise control to ensure the well–being of the fish and their home.

Realising that things cannot be left to take care of themselves the sensible aquarist will develop a method of routine maintenance. **Daily inspection** should be made to ensure that all is well, for no matter how carefully and thoughtfully planned the aquarium or pond may be things do go wrong. There follows a check-list of what should be done, on a routine basis, to maintain a healthy balance of life in aquarium and pond.

### THE AQUARIUM

It is a simple matter to attend to the aquarium once every week:
1. Check plants are alive by gently pulling them; some plants appear to be alive, when their root system is, in fact, dead.
2. Trim off dead or dying foliage.
3. Stir surface of gravel to loosen it and syphon over with a hose–pipe to remove loose sediment. Allow dirty water to discharge into a bucket.
4. Top up aquarium with fresh water, the same temperature as that in the aquarium.
5. Clean front glass of splashes; occasionally it will

also be necessary to remove algae from here. This should be done before syphoning out debris.

THE POND

Apart from the daily inspections, the pond does not require such frequent attention as the aquarium. However, it does benefit from an annual clean-out before the onset of the winter to prevent the possible build up of noxious gases, from rotting material and other causes when the pond freezes over, and so aiding the fish to survive the winter, and emerge in healthy condition.

If the major overhaul is made during the early autumn, it is wise to give a very light clean-up during early spring to remove any winter accumulation of debris. It is surprising the amount of detritus that can be deposited on the bottom of a pond during a period of only six months.

## Cleaning

**Equipment needed:** long-handled net, container for fish, stiff scrubbing brush, utensil for bailing out silt.

**Method**

1. Lower water level to facilitate catching the fish.
2. Carefully place netted fish into containers of clean water, same temperature as in the pond. Remove containers from working area.
3. Remove plant containers from pond and gently hose to clean off blanket weed and sediment. Remove dead leaves and stems and any strands of algae. Cover with wet newspaper and leave them in a cool, sheltered spot to prevent them drying out.
4. Drain off remaining water and bail out silt, keeping watch for any fish that may have buried themselves in the sediment. Dispose of silt in the garden; its evil smell soon goes and it proves a good fertiliser.
5. Scrub and hose pond interior repeatedly to remove sediment and algae, draining accumulated water between flushings. If you have a filter, connect the hose and backflush until water runs clear.

6. Partially refill and empty pond several times to remove as much fine sediment as possible; pond is ready to refill when sediment sinks quickly, leaving water clear.
7. Replace container plants and slowly refill pond with fresh water. If it is a hot day, leave newspaper on plants until water covers them.
8. Inspect fish for signs of disease or parasites. If healthy, return to pond, floating bucket in pond before releasing fish, to equalise water temperatures.

**Winter maintenance**

It is seldom that a pond will freeze solid in winter, provided it has a depth of at least 18 inches (457 mm), due to a peculiar property of fresh water. On cooling, fresh water contracts and becomes denser until it reaches a temperature of 39.2 F ($4°$ C). If cooled further, it begins to expand again and becomes lighter. Thus with the onset of freezing conditions, the colder water from the surface sinks and warmer water from below rises to take its place. This continues until the whole body of water reaches $39.2°F$; further cooling results in the colder water remaining at the top, where it freezes. The deeper water, however, remains at $39.2°F$, while the layer of frozen surface water acts as a blanket and slows down further cooling. Even in the most severe conditions there is usually an unfrozen area of deeper water in which the fish can survive.

**Ice** covering the surface of the pond prevents the escape of noxious gases, and to allow these to escape, a hole must be kept open in the ice. Never break the ice haphazardly because the broken pieces may freeze into an even greater thickness, and blows from a hammer can kill the fish by concussion. It is far safer either to drill 1 inch (25 mm) holes or melt a hole in the ice. Draw off a few inches of water to create an air space below the sheet of ice, then cover the hole with straw or something similar, to prevent cold air freezing the lowered water level. The hole will admit oxygen and allow the gases to escape. Check the hole each day to ensure that it remains open.

Plants need light in order to survive and produce oxygen. If **snow** covers the frozen water surface it will cut out the light and prevent it reaching the plants; this prevents the plants performing their essential function and they may even die. Snow must therefore be swept off the ice every day. The danger of 'winter-kill', as it is known, is greater when snow blankets the ice and prevents the plants receiving sufficient light.

It is possible to purchase specially made 'pond-heaters'. These are very like aquarium heaters, and may be connected to an electricity point. It should be of only sufficient wattage to keep an open hole in the ice during freezing weather, when placed just below the surface of the water; it should not be so high that it prevents the fish hibernating.

# CHAPTER 4

# GOLDFISH

## BACKGROUND

Goldfish belong to the *Cyprinidae*, or Carp Family, and bear the scientific title of *Carassius auratus*; a very plastic species, which, through mutation and manipulation, has developed into many forms, some being quite bizarre, that bear little resemblance to their original wild forebears.

There is some doubt about the earliest date that the goldfish was seriously cultivated, although there is little doubt that it originated in China. There is evidence to prove that the fish was popular and being cultivated, during the Chinese Sung Dynasty, which was around 1000 A.D. During this period Chinese literature contained many references to the goldfish.*

## VARIETIES

Of the many different varieties of fancy goldfish, the following are probably those best known to western aquarists. The varieties can be found in three groups; the well known golden metallic type, which is referred to by the obvious name of **Metallic**; a type known as **Nacreous** in which the fish lacks the metallic shine but exhibits a number of varied colours; the best specimens have a bright blue background over which there are areas of red, yellow, orange, violet, brown and black to a greater or lesser degree. The third group, known as **Matt**, is not considered of any value; it lacks the shine of the first group and has a pink to pinkish-white body.

*See *Fancy Goldfish Culture*, Frank W Orme, Saiga Publishing.

## Common Goldfish:

probably the first deviation from wild type. Attractive feature, the metallic shine of scales. Colour may be reddish–orange, pale orange, yellow or silver, or a combination of these; black, if evident, is a transient colour which, with time, will disappear. Silver areas may also expand until it eventually covers the fish.

## London Shubunkin:

body shape and finnage of Common goldfish, but lacks the shining scales. A nacreous fish, and should carry the colours of that particular group. Some aquarists still refer to the nacreous type fish by the older name calico.

## Bristol Shubunkin:

so called because it was developed by members of the Bristol Aquarist's Society, they also produced the first *show standard* in 1934. Nacreous–type fish; the body slim and streamlined, with high dorsal fin. Main feature: the caudal fin, much larger than usual with large rounded lobes. Other fins equally well developed. Attractive, and probably the most popular, type of fancy goldfish.

## Wakin:

'common goldfish' of Japan. Similar in appearance to Common Goldfish, but has a double caudal fin and twin anal fins.

## Jikin:

'Peacock-tail'; body somewhat like the Wakin but thicker in the belly region. Very old Japanese variety; best specimens have silver body with red lips and fins. Distinguishing feature: caudal fin, which seen from behind is 'X' shaped and attached to a broad peduncle; its axis is almost perpendicular to the axis of body.

## Ryukin:

Japan's most popular variety. Shows first real deviation towards the short, deep–bodied types. Body: short and deepish, often with pronounced hump where back joins head. Fins: longer than those of Common Goldfish; caudal, deeply forked at its edge and divided into two fins; anal fins paired.

## Fantail:

western version of Ryukin. Body: egg–shaped and not as deep as the Ryukin, nor with the hump; finnage, however, very similar. One type has very protruberant eyes, known as telescope–eyed.

## Tosakin:

probably a sport from the Ryukin, which it resembles. Main differences: slightly shallower body, somewhat shorter fins, and a peculiarity of caudal fin. Lower lobes greatly extended with upturned outer edges, so that the fin appears to reverse itself and spread out towards head.

## Comet:

slimmer than Bristol Shubunkin, but with similar finnage, except that the caudal fin is as long as the body, and deeply forked into two ribbon –like extremities.

## Veiltail:

round-bodied variety with two long, fully separated, caudal fins, falling in graceful folds to broad, square-cut lower edge. Anal fin, long and paired; dorsal fin, high and sail-like; remaining fins equally well developed. Both normal and telescope-eyed forms, however, nacreous, normal eyed type is probably most popular with British aquarists.

## Moor:

often wrongly called 'Black-moor', which tends to state the obvious; is only a Moor if it is black. Similar to telescope-eyed Veiltail, with beautiful mantle of deep matt black, giving velvet-like appearance. Colour should extend to the tips of fins, and be free of brassy shine. Always a metallic form, but lacks great reflective lustre.

## Oranda:

generally preferred type; has a shiny metallic scaled body, but in all other respects, identical to Veiltail. Main feature, a peculiarity of head; covered in raspberry-like growth, the 'hood', spreading over the whole of the head bar eyes, mouth and nostrils. Nacreous form sometimes given Japanese name '*Azumanishiki*'; head-growth may be given the Japanese name of '*wen*'.

## Lionhead:

also known by Japanese title of '*Ranchu*' where it is considered to be the 'King of Goldfish.' Short, rather deepish body, broad across the back, with short, strong peduncle supporting twin caudal fins. Fins, short and sturdy; anal fins paired; noticeable lack of dorsal fin. Head covered, like the Oranda, in raspberry-like head-growth.

## Redcap Oranda and Redcap Lionhead:

merely colour variations of their respective variety. Hoods tend to be less well developed and capped by red patch; remainder of fish is metallic silver. The red patch on top of the head gives the fish its name.

## Phoenix:

body midway between that of Common Goldfish and Lionhead. No dorsal fin but other fins compensate by over-development; fins very long; anals paired; double caudal fin deeply forked to give 'ribbon-tail.'

## Pearlscale:

usually silver with large patches of orange-red. Body very fat, with deep belly and flattish back. Fins very similar to Fantail, but caudal fin is not so deeply forked. Main feature, the scales; domed, raised centres, slightly darker margin to the edges and lying in even rows along the body to give a distinct pearl-like effect as they reflect the light.

## Pompon:

closely resembles the Lionhead, but with normal head. Two types: one has full complement of fins, the other has no dorsal fin — British aquarists prefer the latter. Derives name from abnormal enlargement of the tissue dividing the nostrils, forming fleshy lobes, *narial bouquets*, which float before the eyes.

**Celestial:**
    longish bodied variety with finnage somewhat similar to Ryukin.
    Telescope-eyes turn upwards, gazing heavenwards, hence the name.
    No dorsal fin.
**Toadhead:**
    similar to Celestial. Eyes normal, but below each, small bladder-like
    growth making face vaguely toad-like.
**Bubble-eye:**
    like the above variety, but the fluid-filled sacs beneath the eyes much
    larger; as fish swims these bladders, like water-filled balloons, move
    in grotesque manner.
**Meteor:**
    strange egg-shaped variety; no caudal fin; compensated for by over-
    development of other fins.

## Other varieties

It has been estimated that there are more than one
hundred different varieties of fancy goldfish. Many may
never be seen in the west, others may be too grotesque to find
acceptance anywhere other than in their homeland. Such
types described as *Comet-tailed Shubunkins* and/or
*Cambridge Blues* are not recognised goldfish varieties and
will not be found in the tanks of the real hobbyist, they are
names invented for commercial purposes. The *Nymph*, once
recognised as a goldfish variety, is actually a single-tailed
throw-out from a Veiltail spawning. Most serious aquarists
now dispose of such fish at a very young age, for they are of
no value either as future breeding stock or show fish.

## Habitat

Some varieties, such as the Common, London and Bristol
Shubunkins, and the metallic type of Fantail are usually
hardy enough to spend the year in an outdoor pond.
However, due consideration to the size of pond, likely
weather conditions and temperatures must be given. If there
is the slightest doubt then it would be sensible to bring the
fish into a more protected environment before the onset of
the cold months. Other varieties can be allowed to spend the
spring and summer in the pond.

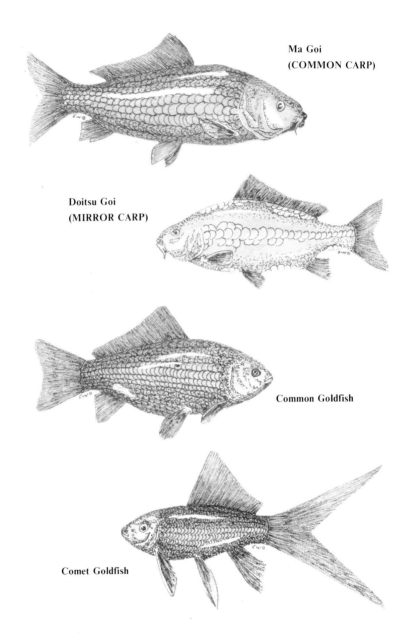

Ma Goi
(COMMON CARP)

Doitsu Goi
(MIRROR CARP)

Common Goldfish

Comet Goldfish

Figure 4.1  **KOI and GOLDFISH**

38

# CHAPTER 5

# KOI

## HISTORY

The Brocaded Carp of Japan is the largest coldwater fish to be kept by the amateur aquarist. Essentially a fish for the pond, it can grow to a length of more than 2 feet (61 cm) if provided with the right conditions.

The koi has been created by the selective breeding of mutated Common Carp, *Cyprinus carpio*. The main distinction between a wild specimen and a domesticated Koi is always the colour and, in some varieties, the scale pattern. In Japan the wild Common Carp is known as *Ma Goi*, whereas the colourful Koi is called *Nishiki Goi*, Nishiki is Japanese for brocaded, or colourful, and Goi means Carp. In the western hemisphere, however, koi has become the most commonly used pronunciation and spelling.

## Introduction to Britain

Early in this century these colourful fish began to spread from their country of origin, Japan, to other parts of the world, where they found many admirers who soon became devotees. It is only since the Second World War, however, that they have really become well known to British fish-keepers. They are now imported in quite large numbers, although the quality often leaves much to be desired, and some are being produced on a smallish scale in this country. No doubt, as more experience is gained, the future will see the fish being bred and raised in increasing numbers by British aquarists.

39

# VARIETIES

Whilst all Koi are of the same species, *Cyprinus carpio*, they are, nevertheless, arranged into different varieties, each depending upon the coloration and scale pattern of the particular fish; these varieties are given Japanese names. The fish may have the normal scale covering of the Common Carp, or it may have the scale pattern of the Mirror Carp or look like the Leather Carp, both being variations of the Common Carp, and will fall into one or other of two groups. If the fish has only one colour it belongs to the **monotone group**, however, when the fish has two or more colours it is placed within the **patterned group**. Commonly used terms, in relation to these Carp, are:

*Akame:*
> meaning red–eyed; indicates albino or semi–albino fish.

*Doitsu:*
> meaning German; applied to Mirror and Leather type Carp because these types originated in Germany and were later crossed with the coloured varieties.

*Ma Goi*: wild Common Carp (*Koi is often changed to Goi if it is preceded by a modifying word*)

*Moyo Goi:*
> patterned type, with a colour additional to the main colour.

*Hi Goi:*
> Hi means red; Hi Goi translates into Red Carp.

*Gin:*
> indicates silver, as in Gin Rin meaning silver scales.

*Kabuto:*
> name given to the helmet worn by the ancient Samurai; used to describe a contrasting colour on the head, when it is thought to resemble a helmet.

## Popular varieties

Kohaku:
> white body upon which is laid a pattern of red; called a Kohaku Kuchibeni, meaning rouged Kohaky when it has red lips, and Kohaku Gin Rin when with silvery scales. The red pattern should be well defined, deep coloured and extensive, especially on the back.

Tancho:
> named after a Japanese white–bodied Crane, which has a red head. White body, red head; ideally the red should appear as a round mark in the centre of the top of the head.

Shiro Muji:
> pure white fish.

**Aka Muji:**

all red fish, the deeper the red the better.

**Shiro Bekko:**

means turtle–shell; a white fish with velvety–black spots.

**Aka Bekko:**

red bodied fish with black spots. Ideal fish has clear black spots on back only, with the lower part completely free of such markings.

**Taisho Sanke:**

named after Emperor Taisho, produced during his time. Sanke means three–coloured. White body over which is laid patterned area of red and black; these colours should not overlap, each to be distinct with sharp edges, well proportioned and symmetrical, confined mainly to dorsal region.

**Ki Goi means a yellow Carp.**

**Showa Sanke:**

Showa refers to the Emperor Showa era during which this variety was produced. Black body with red and white pattern.

**Hi Utsuri:**

black body overlaid with red pattern.

**Ki Utsuri:**

black body with yellow patterns.

**Kin Utsuri:**

black–bodied with scattered golden scales.

**Shiro Utsuri:**

white pattern over black body.

**Cha Koi:**

brown variety.

**Asagi:**

means blue; a blue fish with a reticulated scale pattern.

**Shusui:**

an old variety, produced between 1868 and 1926 by Kichigoro Akiyama senior. Mirror type scales and sky–blue back, becoming lighter on sides. Lower part of body, red.

**Ohgon:**

golden fish covered with glittering scales.

**Orengji Ohgon:**

orange–coloured Ohgon.

**Yamabuki Ohgon:**

glittering scales on bright yellow body. Derives name from yellow flowered Yamabuki plant.

**Hariwake Ohgon:**

resembles ordinary Ohgon, but has areas of greyish colour.

**Purachina Ohgon. Purachina means platinum, indicating a platinum** coloured fish.

**Kin Kabuto:**

devoid of glittering golden scales; only shows gold on head, like a helmet.

**Kin Ki Utsuri:**
yellow and black fish with scattered shiny scales.

There are a number of other colour varieties, however, in every case the colour should be predominantly upon the upper dorsal region of the fish. This is because the fish are pond fish and, therefore, viewed from above.

### ACCOMMODATION

Although young specimens may be kept in an aquarium for a short time they will soon outgrow the restricted quarters, and require the more spacious accommodation of an outdoor pond, if they are to be allowed to reach their full growth potential. Due to the large size of these fish they will require much larger ponds than would be required for goldfish, with a corresponding increase in depth. At least part of the pond should be around 4 feet (122 cm) deep to give adequate winter protection. It is also advisable to employ some form of efficient filtration to preserve the clarity of the water, otherwise it will be found that the water will quickly become discoloured due to the fish stirring up the sediment and any planting medium by their habit of grubbing around for morsels of food. Their large size will also encourage a greater amount of silt than would be produced by goldfish in the same size pond. In the case of Koi it can be said, with some truth, the larger the pond the better it will be for the fish.

Until the fish have become accustomed to the low,

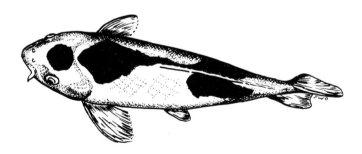

Figure 5.1 **Koi**

42

prolonged temperature of our British winters they should be provided with some protection during the colder months of the year. This caution is especially applicable to newly imported stock, in fact many people make a habit of placing their fish into an indoor pool, such as a collapsible paddling pool, for the winter period. Where possible, however, the aquarist should endeavour to harden the stock slowly to withstand our low temperatures, without removal from the pond. With time, and a greater supply of British produced Koi, it should become easier to keep these Koi throughout the year without having to worry unduly about the cold water conditions.

Carp are capable of jumping, and if placed into strange surroundings, are quite likely to jump out. It is, therefore, a sensible precaution to firmly fix a net over any temporary quarters into which they may be placed, otherwise the fish may leap out and severely damage itself.

## PURCHASING KOI

When buying young specimens of Koi it must be remembered that these fish take up to five years before developing their final colours; in the meantime some colours may fade whilst others darken. It is thus quite difficult to forecast just what the final appearance of even the best coloured young fish may be. Nevertheless, it would seem sensible to choose a vigorous, dark coloured type showing the desired colour pattern, in the hope that it will eventually grow into a good specimen of its particular variety.

# CHAPTER 6

# CHOOSING AND BUYING FISH

Many of the fish which have been described in the previous pages will only be obtainable, if available, from specialised sources, mainly amateur fish breeders, and these sources usually only become known from contact with more experienced aquarists, or through specific enquiry, perhaps to a dealer in pet fish. In this respect it must be mentioned that those who seek the more exotic, or better quality, types of fish must be prepared to pay high prices. Koi can cost around £100 or more, and a good specimen of the more exotic type of fancy Goldfish, it has been said, is worth its weight in gold!

Almost invariably the newcomer to the hobby of fish-keeping will obtain fish from a local pet shop or large departmental store and these outlets will, almost without exception, be offering stock which has been imported from overseas. By the time the fishes reach the retailer they will, usually, be in a very debilitated state and in need of good care, rest and food to aid recovery. Unfortunately, few receive such treatment, thus many die within a short time of being sold.

## PURCHASE

Care and attention should be given to the selection of any fish that is to be purchased. Careful observation and a sharp eye can help to reduce, to a degree, the risk of buying a sick or ailing specimen. If there is the slightest doubt, it is much safer to resist the temptation to buy rather than risk acquiring a fish which is doomed to an early death.

The sensible person will avoid those retailers who allow

their stock tanks to become dirty, overcrowded and, obviously, neglected, and a check should be made to ensure that there are no dead fish in evidence. Assuming that the dealer's tanks are clean, not overcrowded, and are free of dead fish the buyer should consider the contents in greater detail. The fish should be swimming actively, without effort, with all fins held well-spread. The eyes should be bright and clear and the body free of any blemish or inflammation; it must also appear well nourished with no sign of injury or disease.

## Points to look for

Fish to avoid are those which exhibit any of the following: close folded fins; a wasted body that makes the head appear too large; dull cloudy eyes, or eyes with a whitish film over them; split or torn raggedy fins; blood spots or streaks anywhere upon the body or fins; a greyish-white bloom or film that partially obscures the colour on any part of the body or head; scales that seem to be raised instead of lying flat. Any traces of small white 'cotton-wool' tufts of fungus, any minute white spot, pimples, ulcers, or holes, and apparent pieces of 'thread' anywhere on the fish. Fish which make sudden wild dashes and rub themselves upon any firm object, and flicker the fins; fish which have difficulty rising from the bottom, or float like a cork to the surface; fish which swim with a jerky action, or are stationary but appear to 'shimmy'. These are all positive signs of existing and/or future trouble; avoid also any seemingly healthy fish that occupy the same tank. Be cautious at all times; be safe rather than sorry — far better to go away empty-handed to try elsewhere.

## Remember your container

Although most pet dealers, nowadays, put fish into a plastic bag in which the buyer can carry it home, there is always the possibility of an accident. From whatever source the fish is obtained, it pays to take your own container. An extra strong, large water-tight plastic bag will serve for big fish, however, for smaller fish a plastic bucket, with tight fitting lid, is ideal. It is not necessary to have holes in the lid, in fact the holes could prove a nuisance by allowing water to splash through, and it is only necessary to fill the bucket between half and three–quarters full of water. By this method it is possible to carry fish for many miles, safely, without harming them, provided they are not overcrowded.

## Quarantine and introduction of new fish

The thinking aquarist will prepare a container, filled with water, ready to receive the fish before setting out to make the purchase. This is most important where there are already fish, for all new acquisitions must go through a period of at least fourteen days quarantine. During this time any latent ailment should manifest itself, and appropriate action can be taken. Fail to observe this elementary precaution and the healthy stock stands a good chance, sooner or later, of becoming infected with some malady.

Upon arriving home the bucket should have the lid removed, and then be placed near the previously prepared container for an hour or so, to allow the temperatures to equalise. After sufficient time has elapsed, some of the water from the bucket can be poured into the container. Ideally, the mixture of the waters should be approximately fifty per cent of each. This is to ensure that the fish is not given too great a shock if the characters of the waters are very different, for instance, one may be quite hard whilst the other is soft, and a sudden change from one to the other could upset the fish. The fish should then be gently caught and placed into the waiting container where it should remain for, preferably, twenty–eight days, but certainly not less than the fourteen days already mentioned. During this period partial water changes should be made to help the fish adjust to the new water conditions, always making sure that there is no great variation in the water temperatures. During this period of isolation the fish should be fed lightly, to build up its strength, and it should be kept under close observation for any sign of possible trouble. It would also be worthwhile giving the fish one or two disinfectant baths as a precaution against flukes.

If, at the end of the quarantine period, the fish has proved itself to be healthy, it may be placed into its permanent home, be it aquarium or pond. On no account should the fish be tipped straight into the water of its new quarters. The best method is to place the fish, with some of its water, into a shallow container that can be floated upon the water of its new home and left until the water temperatures have equalised. If the container is then gently tipped onto its side the fish will swim out.

## WHEN TO PURCHASE

Without doubt, Spring is the best time of the year to buy fish. The warmer months which lie ahead will encourage the fish to eat and this will promote growth. Knowing the advantages of the warmer conditions, the sensible aquarist will avoid acquiring travel–weakened fish during the colder months, when they will find it harder to recuperate and acclimatise themselves to new conditions.

# CHAPTER 7

## FEEDING

Although mainly vegetarian, the Carp is omnivorous in its eating habits, and there is little in the way of foods that is not acceptable to the Goldfish and Koi. It is a common mistake to believe that pond fish do not require feeding, or, if they do, only at infrequent intervals. When the number of fish kept in the average man–made pond is considered, it will be realised that the population density is usually much higher than would be found in the wild, thus the heavier demand of our 'over–stocked' domestic pond does not allow the supply of natural foods to build up sufficiently to satisfy the fish. It is essential, therefore, that they are fed in the same way as those in the aquarium.

### HOW MUCH TO FEED

The appetites of both Goldfish and Koi are regulated by water temperature. Within reason, the warmer the water the greater their appetite. During the coldest periods they will cease to feed completely, and become semi–dormant. By observation it is possible to regulate the amount of food offered. Rather than giving a large amount at one time, feed a little often. Uneaten food should be removed; it can become a source of water pollution, as it rots and slowly poisons the water.

### Feeding during absence

Many a fishkeeper has arranged for someone to feed the fish whilst they go on holiday, only to return to find the water has become badly polluted, through over–feeding, and that the fish are dead or dying. It is much safer to leave the fish unfed during an absence from home; they will come

48

to no harm if left for one or two weeks, and may well benefit from the period of fasting.

## WHAT TO FEED

The modern commercially manufactured foods, which are available in both flake and pellet form, are very good for general feeding purposes. These foods usually contain 12 per cent protein, 45 per cent carbohydrate, 4 per cent fats, various vitamins and minerals. However, good though they are they should not be fed to the exclusion of other forms of food. Fish, like most creatures, prefer their diet to be varied, as it would be if living under natural conditions.

### Live foods

A welcome change of diet; some of the more easily obtained, or cultivated are:

**Earthworms:**
up to about 2 inches (51 mm) long are most suitable; red or pink-coloured. Chop into pieces small enough for fish to eat easily. Ideal food to bring fish into breeding condition, has long been used by goldfish breeders for this purpose. Can be brought to the surface by watering an area with 2 gallons (9 litres) water with ½ ounce (14g) potassium permanganate dissolved in it; or can be encouraged to gather in a collecting place, e.g. under a piece of black polythene sheet or by placing a piece of sacking upon the ground and keeping it damp with used tea leaves; after a time a number of worms will be available for collection.

**Whiteworm:**
easily cultivated small creamy-white worm; grows to around ¾ inch (19 mm). Most pet fish stores can supply a starter culture. A popular food amongst goldfish enthusiasts because of its ready availability, ease of cultivation, and acceptability by the fish. Cultivation: make a

Figure 7.1    **Whiteworm**

49

lidless wooden box, about 12 inches (305 mm) square, 6 inches (152 mm) deep; half fill with mixture of sterilized loam and peat. The peat should be thoroughly soaked, then squeezed to remove excess water. Make a 50/50 mixture of loam and peat; lightly firm into the box. Take care that no ants or other life are introduced; you can bake the two ingredients before damping and mixing together. Make a shallow hollow in the soil, fill with food; place the worms on top. Cover the soil with a loose fitting piece of glass, to conserve moisture, and the box with a board, to exclude light. For food, worms can be provided with almost any household scraps that can be made into a soft pulp. Place the box in an airy place, temperature about 55° F. (12.8 C). Replenish food supply as it is consumed, or after removing any uneaten spoilt food, until the worms have established a thriving colony. They gather in thick clusters around the food, when it is simple to roll them into a ball and feed them to the fish. Further boxes may be cultured in the same manner by transferring a few of the worms. Usually takes around a month before the worms have increased sufficiently to start feeding them to the fish.

Grindal worms:

slightly smaller worms also cultivated in boxes. The box need be no more than 2 inches (51 mm) deep, with fine granulated peat laid to depth of 1 inch (25 mm), which should be kept distinctly moist, but not soaking wet. Place starter culture into a shallow depression in the compost; add the food, and cover with loose fitting glass lying directly upon the peat. Cover to exclude light. The culture must be kept warm, about 70°F (21°C); most important for success. Food: pre–cooked baby cereal mixed with warm water to a thin paste; when cool spread this thinly over the worms. Feed as often as the food is consumed, they are voracious feeders; with ample food and warmth will multiply quickly. Aerate by turning the peat over with a fork before each feeding, to help prevent sourness.

Micro Worms:

ideal food for small goldfish and koi because of their small size — less than $\frac{1}{8}$ inch (3 mm). To avoid unpleasant smell, and keep the worms thriving, a new culture should be started every 5 – 6 days. Use shallow plastic dishes as containers, with a little pre–cooked cereal, made into a stiff paste, spread thinly over the bottom. Add starter culture by smearing over surface of cooled food. Cover with a sheet of glass and keep at room temperature. After a few days the culture's surface will be seething with tiny worms. Scrape a knife–blade around the inner edge of the dish to collect the worms. After about five days the culture will start to 'go off'. Fresh cultures will need to be started, preferably arranging a slight overlap in time between each one.

*Starter cultures of these cultivated worms can usually be obtained from the larger pet-shops, particularly one who deals in fish and aquarist sundries.*

50

## Daphnia:

commonly known as the *'water-flea'* because of its jerky swimming action; a popular food. Found in stagnant pools and ponds, duck-ponds, farmyard ponds and similar waters; at times visible near pond edges as a moving reddish cloud just under the water surface. To collect use a fine-mesh net; a figure-of-eight movement will quickly collect a quantity if the water contains a fair population. Place collected Daphnia in a bucket of water and carry home with as little delay as possible; tip the catch into a white bowl, so that it can be inspected, and remove beetles, leeches or other suspicious creatures; a surprising number are invariably caught. Daphnia can be purchased from most pet fish dealers if desired.

## Cyclops:

another small food, usually found with Daphnia; useful live food.

## Tubifex:

a small thread-like worm, slightly over 1 inch (25 mm); reddish in colour. Considered by many aquarists to be one of the finest live foods. Usually found in the bottom ooze of highly polluted waters, often near sewerage outfall, where collecting is a filthy and smelly business. Less troublesome to obtain the occasional supply from a pet dealer. For safety, should be kept in slowly running water for a few days, until the internal filth is excreted and so safe for the fish to eat. Be careful; should any escape they will burrow into the bottom covering, of aquarium or pond, and set up a colony. In the aquarium this can become an unsightly nuisance.

## Bloodworms:

the larvae of a midge; easily recognised by its blood-red colour and

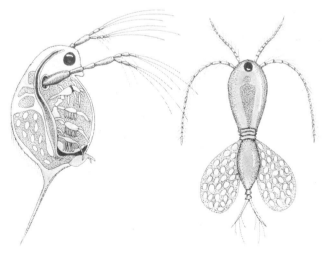

Figure 7.2   **Daphnia**                         **Cyclops**

51

figure-of-eight swimming motion. A very satisfactory food, found in many types of water, even stagnant rain water barrels.

In addition to the live foods it is possible to buy these foods in fresh frozen form which can be safely stored in a deep freezer until required. It is also possible to obtain a variety of live foods in freeze-dried form which can be stored indefinitely. However, neither of these two forms of food are as good as the live creatures, but form a useful standby.

## Other foods

There are a number of other foods which will be accepted, such as canned dog and cat foods, scrambled eggs, finely scraped or chopped liver and heart. Boiled fish will also be eaten, as will soft boiled green peas, cooked or uncooked oatmeal, wheat-germ foods and crumbled wholemeal bread. In fact it will pay to experiment by offering any food which it is thought would be accepted. Large Koi are often fed upon cornflakes, amongst various other unlikely foods.

Figure 7.3 **Tubifex**

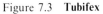

**Worm**

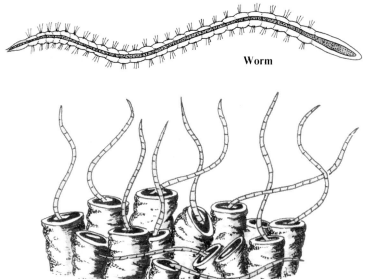

**Part of Mud-Tube Colony**

# CHAPTER 8

## PROBLEMS AND REMEDIES

Observation will help the aquarist to recognise the onset of trouble before it can get out of hand; by recognising the early signs and taking prompt action many common problems can be prevented. Any change in the behaviour of fish warrants further investigation as does any alteration in the colour, smell or clarity of the water. The following is a list of these common problems, and their remedies:

WATER POLLUTION

**Signs:**
strong, unpleasant smell or milkiness of water — healthy water smells pure and has slight amber tint. Fish mouthing at water, quickly returning if disturbed.

**Causes:**
overfeeding, metals in contact with water, especially copper, overcrowded conditions causing lack of oxygen. Laburnum, holly, rhododendron leaves/ berries falling into the water.

**Remedies:**
change water if cloudy or bad smelling. Do not over- feed and remove uneaten food. Do not overcrowd; remember fish to water surface ratio. Avoid contact of metals and poisonous plants.

DISEASES

Fall into two groups, parasitic and non-parasitic, one causing the other. It is difficult to distinguish between the two.

**Signs:**
Sudden loss of appetite; hiding near bottom; difficulty in swimming normally; close folded fins; swimming in circles; shimmying movements; bobbing to surface like a cork; inability to rise easily from the bottom; gulping

air at water surface; scratching upon firm objects and sudden wild dashes; inflamed areas on body or fins; bloated appearance with protruding scales; clouding of eyes or body colours; small white spots, pimples, ulcers or cotton–wooly tufts of fungus; abnormally fast breathing, swollen gills, protruding eyes.

**Causes:**

bad management; cross infection between fish; failure to quarantine; rough handling and accidents.

### Common diseases and parasites

The following lists some of the more common diseases and parasites, and also suggests treatments. The reader is, however, cautioned that the utmost care should be exercised when subjecting fish to any of the treatments. Never exceed the stated strength or duration of the various chemical treatments, and watch the fish closely. If it becomes distressed, remove it to fresh water immediately. Treatment should be continued, in a weakened bath, only after it has fully recovered from the effect of the stronger solution.

**Fungus:**

a common complaint attacking weak or injured fish. Has the appearance of greyish–white tufts of cotton wool. Spores of this fungus (*Saprolegnia*) are present in all waters, but will not harm healthy, uninjured fish. Two methods of treatment, with salt baths of different strengths. The salt should be rock or cooking salt, or better still marine salt, but not table salt, which contains additives.

1.    Prepare a bath containing 5 oz (142 g) salt to each gallon (4.5 l) water; stir until salt has dissolved completely. Place fish into bath for 30 minutes, but watch for signs of distress. Repeat treatment each day until cured.

2.    A safer bath, of longer duration: dissolve 1 oz (28 g) salt into each gallon of water, into which the fish is placed and left. The following day remove half the water and replace with a solution of 2 oz (5 6 g) per gallon. Third day, again remove half the water and replace with water containing salt at the same strength as on previous day. Leave the fish in this solution until cured, then remove one third of the salt water and replace with fresh, untreated water. Repeat for the next three days; the fish can then be returned to the aquarium or pond.

**Fin Congestion:**

generally due to chilling or poor living conditions. Treat the fish to the long term bath, as described for Fungus; make sure that the fish is treated more carefully in the future. In this complaint the fins, especially the caudal fin, become streaked with red blood veins.

54

## Fin Rot:

apt description of malady; fins become torn and ragged, and because the tips are attacked by bacteria, fungus often sets in as secondary complaint. A serious disease that requires immediate treatment. Chilling and dirty conditions are major causes. Two remedies can be employed: 1. Long-term saline bath, if this fails try, 2. mix 1 ml of *Phenoxethol* in 99 ml of water, stir 10 ml of this solution thoroughly into each pint of water as a treatment bath, and place the fish in it for seven days — if it has not recovered within that time, prepare a fresh bath and place the fish in this for a further seven days.

## Slime Disease:

can remain latent when the fish is healthy, but strike when resistance is lowered; more likely to attack aquarium than pond fish. Colours of the fish appear pale under a thin, greyish film of thickened mucus, those affected can be cured by either of the salt-bath treatments described for fungus. If necessary the treatment can be repeated after a two day interval.

## White Spot:

common name for *Ichthyophthrius*, a protozoan parasite causing tiny white blisters, like grains of salt, to appear on body and fins. Can kill, so prompt treatment is required. Prepare stock solution of 1 gm medical quality Methytlene Blue mixed into 100 cc hot water; use at the rate of 4 cc to each gallon of water, mixing thoroughly. Infected fish can be kept in the bath for an indefinite period until blue colour clears from the water; the period can be shortened by increasing the water temperature to about 75° F. (23.9°C.). To be safe continue treatment for a few days after all spots have disappeared.

## Fluke:

may attack either gills or skin of fish; tiny parasites; may just be visible to the naked eye. Can be introduced with infected fish or live-foods obtained from a source containing infected fish. When gills are infected fish breathes more rapidly than normal, and gills are pale in colour, stretched wide open as the fish breathes. Skin fluke causes an increase in mucus, making the colours appear pale; the fins may droop and become ragged. There may be small blood spots or inflamed areas. Most obvious sign of a possible attack by either, probably both, of these parasites is sudden wild dashes and flicking movements of the fish as it rubs against firm objects to ease irritation. Treat with ammonia. Prepare stock solution by adding 10 parts ammonia to 90 parts water; mix 45 cc of this solution with each gallon water, and place the fish into the bath for no longer than 20 minutes. Alternatively, make stock solution of 1 part *Formalin* to 99 parts water, and add at the rate of 165 cc to each cubic foot of water (or $6\frac{1}{4}$ gallons (28.4 litres)) and leave fish in bath until cured. The water temperature should be raised to about 65° F. (18°C.) to avoid secondary infection by fungus.

*Argulus:*
    a round, flattish creature; can be introduced with live–foods obtained
    from wild, natural waters. Commonly known as 'Fish-louse'; large
    enough to be seen easily. Attaches itself to the fish and feeds upon the
    blood. Remove by rubbing it off, or use forceps to pull it from the fish.
*Lernaea:*
    more commonly known as 'Anchor worm' although, in fact, not a
    worm. Buries itself into the body of fish, but leaves the rear part
    exposed, looking like a piece of cotton attached to fish. To remove,
    hold fish in a wet net, and touch the parasite with a fine brush dipped in
    strong dark potassium permanganate solution; should kill the creature
    and allow it to be pulled from the fish with forceps.

**Air Embolism:**
    results in bubbles appearing in the fins, due to an excessive amount of
    oxygen in the water which causes over–saturation of oxygen in the
    fishes' blood. To cure, gradually change half of the water, or place
    affected fish into fresh water. Avoid the problem, if possible, by
    shading water during brightest and warmest days. Under the influence
    of sunshine plants and algae give off oxygen, too much can result in
    this condition.

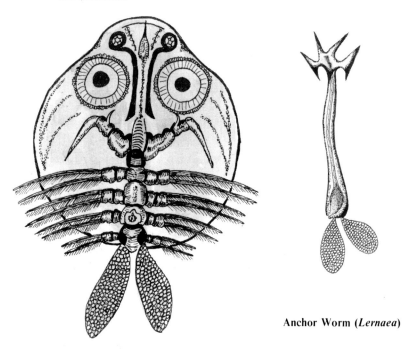

Anchor Worm (*Lernaea*)

Figure 8.1    **Fish Louse (*Argulus*)**

**Disorders of the swim-bladder:**
it is possible for a fish to inherit a swim-bladder problem, but more likely it arises through mismanagement, incorrect feeding, i.e. too much dried food, rapid temperature fluctuations, chilling or prolonged low temperatures. Deep bodied varieties of fancy goldfish can be prone to swim-bladder troubles unless care is taken; once the problem prevents the fish swimming normally there is little chance of recovery. Affected fish may exhibit any of the following signs: floating to surface like a cork; difficulty rising from the bottom, to which it sinks stone-like; inability to maintain balance, possible floating or lying in an upside down position.

**Shimmies:**
due to chilling or prolonged low temperature. Fish stays in one place but swings body in shimmying movement. Raise water temperature slightly until fish recovers, then gradually reduce back to normal temperature.

**Indigestion:**
result of feeding too much dried food for too long. Although not serious, can lead to the above complaint unless treated. Starve fish for 7 days, then feed live Daphnia or chopped earthworms as a laxative. Vary future diet by including more soft and live foods.

## Preventative measures

There are other complaints, however, those mentioned are possibly the most common. Careful management and the strict quarantine of all new fishes will do much to preserve the healthy state of fish. Prompt action can help to avoid any minor outbreak of a complaint developing into something more serious — possibly becoming an epedemic. When treating a fish always note its reaction, for some cannot tolerate the treatment as well as others, and be prepared to give slightly longer treatment in a weakened bath. Never try to speed up a cure by overdosing, this could result in the death of the fish.

Whenever a tank has contained diseased fish, or parasite infested stock, it should be disinfected before any of the inmates are returned. The easiest way to accomplish this is to dissolve potassium permanganate in hot water and then stir into the tank water, turning it a deep purple colour. Leave for 48 hours before thoroughly swilling out and replacing with fresh water. Any plants should be removed before the chemical is added otherwise they will be killed.

## Commercial treatments

For those who do not feel too certain about making up their own treatment baths, there are a number of commercially prepared treatments which, if used according to the manufacturer's directions, are very good. However, it must be stressed that none of the various treatments should be given mixed, as a single bath. If different treatments are required, for any reason, the fish should spend 24 hours in fresh water between treatments.

## PREDATORS

The indoor aquarium is less frequently affected by predators than the outdoor pond, and those found in the aquarium are introduced with live food from natural ponds. One remedy against large predators visiting the pond is to stretch a small mesh net over the pond. The following lists those smaller predators that are harder to guard against, and should be killed when seen:

**Alder–Fly:**
> familiar sight around lakes, ponds and streams during May and June. Larvae spend around two years in the water, crawling over bottom mud. Brown in colour; powerful mandibles; grow to length of 25 mm – 1 inch; will attack any smaller creature.

**Dytiscus:**
> commonly known as Great Diving Beetle; probably best known of the predatory water beetles. Olive–brown with yellow margin around thorax and wing–cases. Maximum length 35 mm (1.4 inches); ferociously carnivorous, readily attacking creatures much larger than itself. Larvae are perhaps even more vicious than adult; grow to about 50 mm (almost 2 inches). Seize their victim in powerful sickle–shaped mandibles and pump digestive fluid into its body, before sucking out the dissolved flesh to leave only the empty skin. Larval period lasts for approx. 1 year.

**Water Boatmen:**
> a common sight in ponds, where they rest at water surface in upside down position. Grow to approx. 15 mm (0.6 inch) and swim on their backs with two long oar–like legs outstretched. Will attack creatures larger than themselves.

**Dragonfly Nymph** (larval stage):
> has 'mask' formed from the third pair of jaws being fused into a moveable structure with strong curved claws. When at rest mask is folded back under head, however, when prey comes within striking distance mask is shot forward to seize victim in vice–like grip — after which it is slowly eaten. Normally sluggish, it lurks in wait for victims.

58

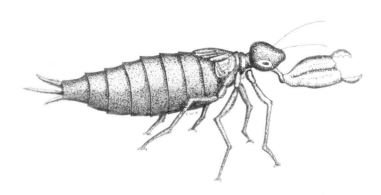

Figure 8.2 **Dragonfly Larva**

Can reach size of around 50 mm.

**Water Scorpion:**

like a dead leaf; flat, and dark brown in colour. Length 30 mm (1.2 inches) or more. Hides in mud of shallow water. Front legs are modified to enable it to grasp its prey firmly to suck juices from the body.

**Water Stick Insect:**

related to the Water Scorpion, it has similar habits. Stick–like body; grows to around 65 mm (2.5 inches). Little can be done to prevent it entering the pond, for parents can fly from one pond to another to deposit eggs. The beetles can also fly — often at night.

**Hydra:**

of danger only to very small fish fry, which it captures in its tentacles. When extended, resembles a tiny sea–anemone, but if disturbed will quickly contract into jelly–like blob. Usually plentiful in natural, weedy waters, often being introduced into the aquarium or pond with plants or live–foods gathered from such places. Can become an unsightly pest in the aquarium and should be removed by stirring 1 teaspoonful ammonia into each 4 gallons water. Fish must be removed prior to adding the ammonia otherwise they will die; also harms plants. After 48 hours aquarium can be emptied and flushed out to remove all traces of ammonia, then refill and replace fish. If necessary repeat treatment until *Hydra* are completely wiped out.

**Planarians:**

flat, limbless creatures of whitish colour which crawl over the plants, or on the glass of the aquarium. These flatworms are harmless to adult

59

fish but may eat fish eggs. No satisfactory way of removal except to strip the aquarium down, and thoroughly disinfect and clean the tank, gravel and plants.

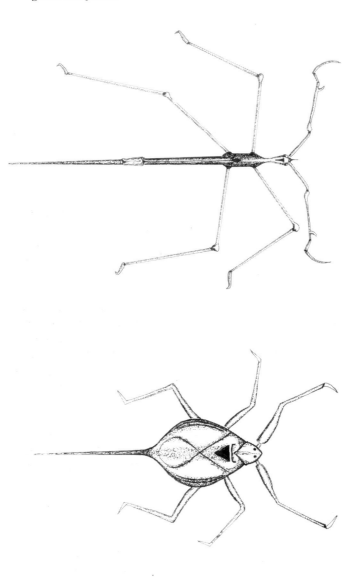

Figure 8.3   **Water-Stick Insect (*top*), and Water Scorpion**

# CHAPTER 9

## FISH BREEDING

### Breeding condition

In order for fish to spawn they must be in breeding condition. In order to bring the fish into breeding condition they must be well fed and in a state of good health; this can be achieved by providing clean living quarters and offering plenty of live–foods; chopped earthworms have long been recognised as one of the best foods for conditioning. The water temperature also has a bearing upon the condition of the fish, therefore the best time to consider trying to encourage a spawning is when the water temperature has risen to around at least 60° F. (15.6° C.), thus springtime becomes the obvious choice.

As the female develops, she will usually become noticeably plump, and the male will assume his breeding characteristics; small white pinhead–size pimples, known as tubercles, which are developed upon the front rays of the pectoral fins, the gill covers and elsewhere around the head region. Both sexes will swim in an alert manner with their fins well spread and exhibit all those signs which are so obviously signs of good health. At this stage it will be reasonable to assume that they have reached that peak of condition known as 'breeding condition', and an attempt can be made to spawn them, unless the spawning is to be allowed to take place in the pond.

### Spawning

A tank, the larger the better, should be thoroughly cleaned, filled with fresh water, but nothing else, and placed in a position which allows the morning sunshine to reach it. At one end of this tank bunches of really well cleaned fine–

leaved plants should be placed, in which the fish will spawn. Alternatively, lengths of nylon knitting wool can be made into mops and, after being boiled to remove any free dye, hung in the tank. This latter method has the advantage of ensuring that no snails or other pests are likely to be introduced. The tank can then be left for a time to allow any excess oxygen to disperse from the water, and for the water temperatures of the tank to adjust to that of the aquarium that contains the fish.

When all is ready, the male can be placed gently into the prepared breeding tank. If this is done during the evening it will allow the fish to settle down to the strange surroundings during the night. The following evening the female can be placed with the male. If, within a short time, he shows interest and begins to follow the female around, perhaps occasionally nudging her, it is possible that by the following morning they may be spawning. However, if this does not occur they should not be interfered with, but allowed to remain together for a few days and fed with earthworms.

Figure 9.1
**Nacreous Lionheads Spawning.** The male fish pushes and lifts the plump female with his head towards the nylon wool spawning mops.

Should the fish refuse to spawn, repeat the conditioning procedure; it may help if the sexes can be separated for a time.

The true spawning drive cannot be mistaken. The male will vigorously chase the female around the tank, continually bumping her, until she swims into the spawning area. There she will release a number of eggs, which the male will fertilise by releasing milt into the water, and the fertilised eggs will fall into the plants, or mops, to which they adhere. This wild chase may last for several hours, during which time the fish are oblivious to everything except the urge to spawn. The eggs are about the size of a pin–head and a translucent clear to amber colour. Infertile eggs will turn white and develop fungus.

It is generally advisable to remove the fish around mid–day and return them to their tank, where they should be well fed to assist them to recover their strength. If left in the breeding tank they will start to eat the eggs once they have finished spawning.

In order to shorten the hatching time it is usual to raise the water temperature to 75°F. (25° C.), which will encourage the eggs to hatch in about three days. Under natural conditions the hatching period could be seven or more days, during which time many pests would have the opportunity to attack.

In the event that the fish are to be allowed to spawn in the pond, as may well be necessary in the case of large Koi, some means of trapping the eggs must be supplied. A close watch should be kept to ensure that the spawning is not missed, and eggs gathered as the spawning takes place. The eggs can then be placed into a hatching tank, and the temperature slowly raised, as already described.

At first the newly hatched *alevins* will look like small glass splinters, and will hang from the spawning medium, the tank glass and near the water surface. At this stage it is imperative that they are not disturbed, otherwise they may have difficulty in rising to the water surface again, a feat which they must accomplish in order to fill their swim–bladders and so become free swimming.

**Feeding the fry**

Once they have become free–swimming, fine food must be supplied, in sufficient quantity to keep their stomachs filled. Most fish breeders use newly hatched Brine Shrimps for the first few days. Vials of Brine Shrimp eggs can be purchased from most aquarium–fish dealers, and full hatching instructions are included. Upon this easily cultured, tiny live–food the small fish will make quite rapid growth. Another method is to hard boil an egg and then place a very small piece of the yolk only, in a handkerchief; this is then squeezed through the handkerchief to form a fine cloud in the water, however, great care must be taken not to overdo it, otherwise the water will quickly become polluted and the small fish will die.

As the fry grow they can gradually be weaned onto very small Daphnia, finely crushed commercial flake food and mashed whiteworms. Slowly increase the size of the food to keep pace with the rate of growth of the fishes, until they have developed sufficiently to accept normal foods.

**Raising**

During the growing period they must be continuously sorted to remove all deformed and inferior specimens. They must also be given plenty of space in which to grow if they are to develop in a satisfactory manner. Food and space are the two essentials in successfully raising young fish — if either is in short supply the fish will suffer. Too often the novice tries to raise too many young fish and ends up with a lot of undersized, poor quality young; far better to concentrate upon raising around half–a–dozen well grown youngsters that do their breeder credit.

The water temperature, after hatching, should be slowly reduced until, by mid-August, heating is dispensed with and the young fish allowed to harden to the natural temperature fluctuations of a normal coldwater environment. In fact, if they have grown large enough, say about 1 inch, they can be hardened off before August and placed into an outdoor pond, provided the pond does not contain any large fish that would be capable of eating them.

Young fish that hatched out up to late May should have reached a length of around 2 inches (50.8 mm) by the end of October, and at that size can safely remain outdoors during the winter, however, if they are smaller then, for safety, they should be brought indoors until the warmer months return.

**Breed pure fish**

Finally, little purpose is served by inter–breeding different species. Although it is possible to cross the Koi with the Goldfish, the offspring are unlikely to be more than unwanted curiosities. Equally, the breeder who cross–breeds different goldfish varieties undoes the work of many genera-tions and produces nothing more than unwanted 'mongrel' fish. It should be the aim of all fish breeders to produce pure, quality stock and always endeavour to improve the existing types by considered selective breeding.


## COMMERCIAL BREEDING

The novice fishkeeper, once the fish have been bred and a number of young fish successfully raised, begins to think about the disposal of any surplus fish; often with the idea of making a profit. However, it will soon be realised that such hopes are unlikely to be fulfilled.

**Selling to pet shops**

Possible a local pet shop will be prepared to buy any unwanted stock, however, the fish will need to be well grown. Even so the price offered will, generally, not be very great and may not even compensate for the cost of feeding and growing the fish. The breeder may well feel aggrieved to discover, subsequently, that the dealer himself demands a very much higher figure for the cheaply bought fishes, but the dealer has to buy in his stock at a price which allows him to resell at attractive prices to cover his overheads. It must also be remembered that very often imported fish can be bought in cheaper than home–bred stock, although the latter may be hardier, and of better quality.

## Limitations on the amateur

The amateur who has only a couple of small aquaria and a pond must realise that such restricted accommodation cannot lend itself to anything other than the production of a few fish. To raise even one type of fish in worthwhile quantities needs more equipment, tank and pond space than the average aquarist usually has available. That is not to say that amateurs cannot provide themselves with sufficient fish breeding space; many do, however, even they find the market very limited and only expect to cover part of their seasonal expenses from the sale of young fish.

## Goldfish breeding

At the present time goldfish enthusiasts form the larger proportion of coldwater fish breeders. Generally they have an outdoor building, often similar to a greenhouse, in which they have a number of large aquaria — known as the fish-house. In addition there are outside ponds for raising the young fish and holding adult stock. It is noticeable that most of these enthusiasts tend to specialise in only one or two varieties of fancy goldfish, which they line–breed to a pre-determined programme. They produce their stock in much the same way that other pedigree animals are produced; by carefully selected breeding. Unfortunately, the goldfish does not breed true to type, and no matter how skillful the breeder may be, many of the young will be of inferior quality, due to their tendency to revert, in some degree, back to the wild type fish. The goldfish breeder must use past experience and knowledge in an effort to counteract this, and so improve the quality of those which do come true to type.

## Showing

Most successful fish breeders are also exhibitors at the various fish shows. By placing their fish on the show bench, in competition with others, they advertise their stock by allowing others to see and assess the quality. Success on the show bench not only acknowledges the quality of the exhibit, but also adds value to it. As a direct result of this, the

66

breeder may well receive a number of enquiries from people interested in obtaining fish from the same strain. It is from these fellow hobbyists that the best prices will be obtained, for they are well aware of the value of a decent quality fish and of the costs involved in producing fish of a saleable size. They also know what a small percentage of worthwhile young are likely to be found in even the largest spawning from a pair of first–class fish.

## Advertising and transport

Some fish breeders advertise that they have fish for sale in the classified columns of one or other of the hobby magazines, thus reaching interested parties far beyond the breeder's locality. When replying, the fish should be accurately and truthfully described, noting age and size. A suggested day and time of despatch by passenger train should be made, with a warning that no guarantee will be given, or any responsibility taken, for the safe, live delivery of the fish. The fishes should be placed into a plastic bucket, with a watertight lid securely fastened, and clearly labelled to their destination. The bucket should also inform handlers that it contains *Live Fish*. The carriage charge will be based upon the total weight of the bucket and the distance it has to travel to its destination. The purchaser must be informed, in good time, of the time of arrival, so that the fish can be collected without delay. This is usually done by telegram. Thus when replying to any out–of–town enquiries, apart from describing the fish and stating the price required, the cost of a telegram and the estimated cost of carriage should also be mentioned.

## Pre–purchase viewing

Most people will wish to see the fish before deciding to buy, and the fish breeder must be prepared to allow potential buyers to view the stock. If the overall quality of the stock is good, their health sound and their living quarters clean there is nothing to fear from allowing an inspection. It will then only require a fair price to be asked in order to make a sale. Satisfy the buyer and word will soon spread to others.

# CHAPTER 10

## FISH SHOWS

Although many aquarists disapprove of public fish exhibitions, the vast majority derive a great deal of pleasure from visiting the competitive fish shows. These exhibitions are events which enthusiasts look forward to with anticipation. To the breeder they provide a means of having an independent assessment made by a qualified judge of the quality of the exhibited fish. The fish can be compared against others of the same variety and personal conclusions drawn as to how much progress has been made in the improvement of the exhibitor's stock; thus competition provides the incentive to greater endeavour.

### Benefits of showing

There are other advantages to the open show, apart from the element of competition. It enables experienced breeders to display their fish, and thus find a market for their stock, and the novice to see top quality fish, meet experienced fishkeepers and gain valuable advice from them. It brings together enthusiasts from other parts of the country, and so allows new friendships to be formed, ideas exchanged and knowledge imparted. It provides publicity for the hobby by attracting the general public, teaches the novice to distinguish a good fish from an inferior one, and provides a meeting place for all who enjoy a similar interest.

### THE SHOW

The majority of these events are one day affairs (usually held in a church hall or some similar venue) and cater, in the main, for the tropical fish, with a few classes for fancy goldfish and other coldwater fish. Some, however, such as the National Shows are larger, lengthier events (usually three days) and are held in various parts of the United Kingdom. At these prestige exhibitions it is usual to find the trade strongly represented by their many trade stands.

## Specialist shows

Of premier interest to coldwater fishkeepers are the specialist shows for Fancy Goldfish and Koi. These attract the country's best-known exhibitors, many travelling a considerable distance to enter their fish. The judges at these shows are invariably experienced fishkeepers with a sound knowledge of the finer points of a good fish. They need a sharp eye, for the quality of the fish can make judging very difficult; the difference between a first and second place award may be little more than a half-point in the marking of the judge.

Due to the large size of some of the Koi exhibits, the organisers of these shows arrange for large portable vats, placed outside, to be filled with water ready to accommodate the entries as they arrive. Generally the shows are held in a park-like setting and patrolled by official stewards who, whilst keeping a watchful eye on the fish, are prepared to answer any questions that are put to them.

The specialist shows for Fancy Goldfish are held indoors, where the exhibitor finds the organisers have arranged ready filled tanks, with class labels, awaiting the entries.

In order to compete in these open shows it is necessary to submit an entry form, together with the correct fees, some weeks prior to the event. This enables the show committee to arrange for a sufficient number of containers to be made ready for the exhibitors' entries. Upon arrival at the venue, the exhibitor presents a copy of the entry form to one of the official stewards before being shown which containers the fish are to be placed in.

## Mixed shows

The smaller, mixed shows will generally accept entries on the day of the show. The exhibitor, however, should make sure that the show contains a class for the particular fish he hopes to enter.

Unlike the specialist shows, the exhibitor in these mixed events must supply a show tank in which to exhibit the fish. The usual size is 10 inches long x 8 inches deep x 6 inches wide (254 mm x 203 mm x 152 mm), for single fish, and must be clean. All panels must be clear, and no plants or other adornments are allowed. It is the task of the exhibitor to fill the tank with water, place the fish into it, and affix the identification label to the top left corner of the front panel. The tank is then handed to a steward to be placed on the show bench. At the close of the show, the exhibitor removes the fish and empties the tank.


## SHOWING PROCEDURES

At no time after benching, at any of the shows, is the exhibitor allowed to touch the fish without first obtaining official sanction, nor may a fish be removed until after the show has finished, unless supervised by a steward. This is, of course, the exhibitors' safeguard against the possible theft of a fish. Such incidents, although rare, do happen, and, whilst accepting no responsibility, most show organisers try to guard against such things happening.

Before entering any show a copy of the **show schedule** should be obtained (the various shows are listed within the pages of the hobby magazines, together with the address of the show secretary). Study the rules and classes carefully. Decide which of the classes to enter. See whether it is necessary to supply a show tank; it is foolish to carry a fish to a show and then find there is no tank to put it in. Fill in the entry form and return it in good time (unless entries are accepted on the day of the show) together with the correct entry fee. Note the times allowed for benching the fish, and arrive well within the stated hours — late entries may be refused admission. Remember that the show rules are binding upon the exhibitor, who should be aware of the conditions governing the show. Take care that the fish are entered and benched in the correct class, as a fish entered in the wrong class will usually be disqualified.

Having placed the fish in its correct position, and, if in a tank, wiped away any smears from the front glass, it becomes a matter of patiently waiting for the completion of judging. The exhibitor should be prepared to accept the judge's decision as final. The fact that a fish has been lucky enough to obtain an award at a previous show does not mean that it will do as well on its next outing; a different judge may spot a fault that was missed on the previous occasion, the competition may be keener, or the fish may be off–colour. It must be remembered that the judges do their utmost to allot the awards fairly, in an impartial and conscientious manner, to those which they consider are the better fish.

## Learn from shows

If, upon returning, it is found that no award has been gained, study those which have been more fortunate and note the differences that have made them the better specimens. Approach an experienced exhibitor and tactfully ask for the good and bad points of the unsuccessful fish to be pointed out. Do not dispute if the criticism appears harsh — accept it gracefully, and learn. Always be prepared to listen to sound advice from experienced aquarists, and ignore the ramblings of fools.

## METHODS OF EXHIBITING KOI AND GOLDFISH

The Fancy Goldfish is displayed in a tank, which allows it to be seen from all angles, and is judged against a set of specific 'show standards'. In Japan, however, the fish is judged from above, as it would be seen when swimming in the pond, and this is the method which is employed to judge Koi. This may at first seem strange. In fact it is very sensible to judge Koi in this way, for they are primarily pond fish, growing much too large for the average amateur aquarium. Also, being bred as pond fish, the Japanese breeders have concentrated the colour patterns mainly upon the dorsal area of the fish for clear viewing. The Fancy Goldfish is known for its diversity of body shape and finnage, and this can only be seen to advantage in the aquarium. The Koi, on the other hand, is bred purely for its colour patterns; in all other respects it has remained almost identical to its wild carp forebears and gains nothing by being placed in an aquarium.

# APPENDIX

## SOCIETIES

The **Goldfish Society of Great Britain** (includes overseas membership)
**The Ranchu Society**
**Bristol Aquarist's Society**
**The Northern Goldfish and Pondkeepers Society**
**Association of Midland Goldfish Keepers**
**The British Koi-Keeper's Society**
**The Yorkshire Koi Society**
**The Midland Koi Association**

The names and addresses of the secretaries of the respective societies can be obtained by writing to either of the hobby magazines, including an SAE. It is also possible to set up your own society, if there are none in the locality, by contacting local fanciers.

## BOOKS

Those recommended are:
*The Goldfish* G. J. Hervey, F.Z.S., and J. Hems, Faber & Faber, London
*The Book of the Garden Pond* G. J. Hervey, F.Z.S., and J. Hems, Faber & Faber, London
*Goldfish Guide* Dr. Yoshiichi Matsui, Pet Library Ltd, U.S.A.
*Coldwater Fishkeeping* Arthur Boarder, Buckley Press, Brentford
*Fancy Goldfish Culture* Frank W. Orme, Saiga Publishing Company Ltd., Hindhead
*Goldfish and Koi in your Home* Dr. Herbert R. Axelrod and William Vorderwinkler, T.F.H. Publications, U.S.A.
*Water Garden* Gordon T. Ledbetter, Alpha Books
*Encyclopaedia of Live Foods* Charles O. Masters, T.F.H. Publications Ltd., U.S.A.
*Encyclopaedia of Water Plants* Dr. Jiri Stodola, T.F.H. Publications Ltd., U.S.A.
*Freshwater Life* John Clegg, Federick Warne, London
*Cyclopaedia of Coldwater Fish and Pond Life*, Frank W. Orme, Saiga Publishing Co. Ltd., Hindhead

# MAGAZINES

***The Aquarist and Pondkeeper*** — details from; The Editor, The Butts, Half Acre, Brentford, Middlesex

***Practical Fishkeeping Monthly:*** EMAP National Publications, Bretton Court, Bretton, Peterborough